MW00977946

The Best Ever Book of Bible Activities: New Testament

Published in Grand Rapids, Michigan by Baker Book House.
Printed in the United States of America.

ISBN 0-8010-4405-7

1 2 3 4 5 — 01 00 99 98

JESUS' ANCESTORS

Matthew 1:1-17

Use the clues in the box below to complete the crossword.

1. God asked the man to sacrifice his son.
2. The name of the son who was going to be sacrificed.
3. He helped Ruth find food, then he married her.
4. King Saul liked to hear him play his harp. He wrote many of the Psalms in our Bible.

The first chapter of Matthew traces Jesus' relatives all the way back to Abraham. The prophets wrote that Jesus would be related to King David. The list of names in Matthew shows that King David was Jesus' ancestor.

answers
Abraham
Isaac
Boaz
David

A SPECIAL BIRTH ANNOUNCEMENT

Luke 1:57-66

Break the secret code to find out what the angel said.

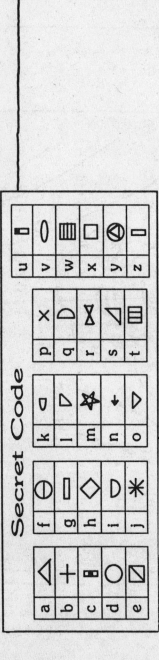

Secret Code

a	◁	f	⊖	k	▽	p	✕	u	▯
b	✛	g	▭	l	△	q	◿	v	⬭
c	▤	h	◇	m	✳	r	⋈	w	☰
d	◯	i	▷	n	↓	s	◁	x	▢
e	◹	j	✳	o	▷	t	▦	y	⊘
						z	▯		

Zechariah and Elizabeth didn't have any children and now they thought they were too old. But one day when Zechariah was in the temple an angel gave him a special message.

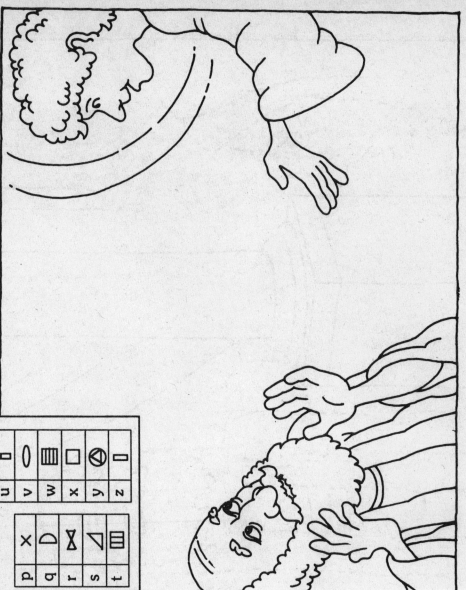

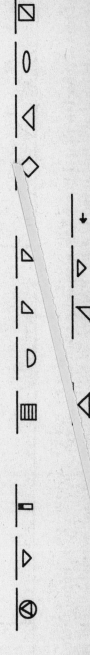

ZECHARIAH LOSES HIS VOICE

Luke 1:5-25

Trace over the dotted lines to complete this picture.

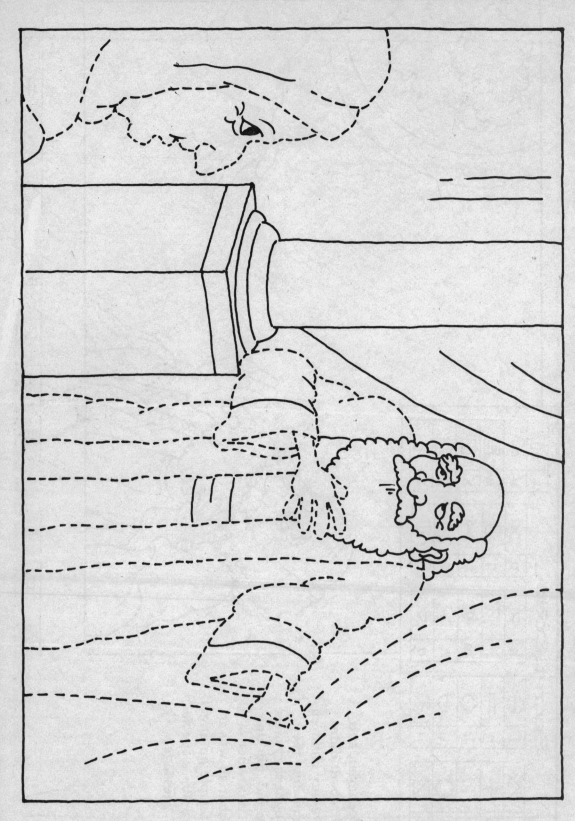

The angel told Zechariah that a baby boy would be born to Elizabeth. They were to name their son John. Zechariah was so amazed that he didn't believe the angel at first. Because of his unbelief Zechariah wasn't able to speak until the baby was born.

An Angel's Message for Mary

Luke 1:26–38

Beginning at #1, connect the dots to complete the picture.

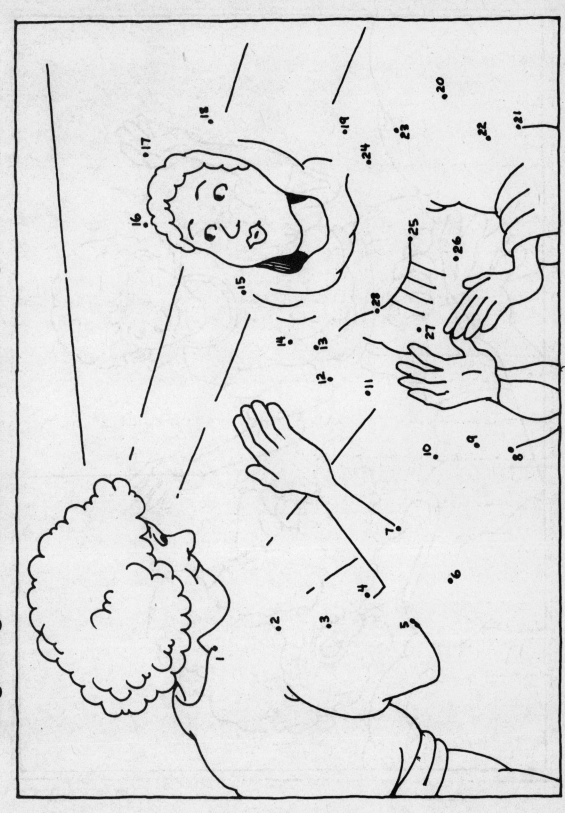

Six months after the angel talked to Zechariah, a young girl in Nazareth saw an angel, too. The angel told Mary that she was going to have a baby, too. Her baby would be the son of God.

JESUS' BIRTH IS ANNOUNCED TO JOSEPH

Matthew 1:18-25

Color this picture.

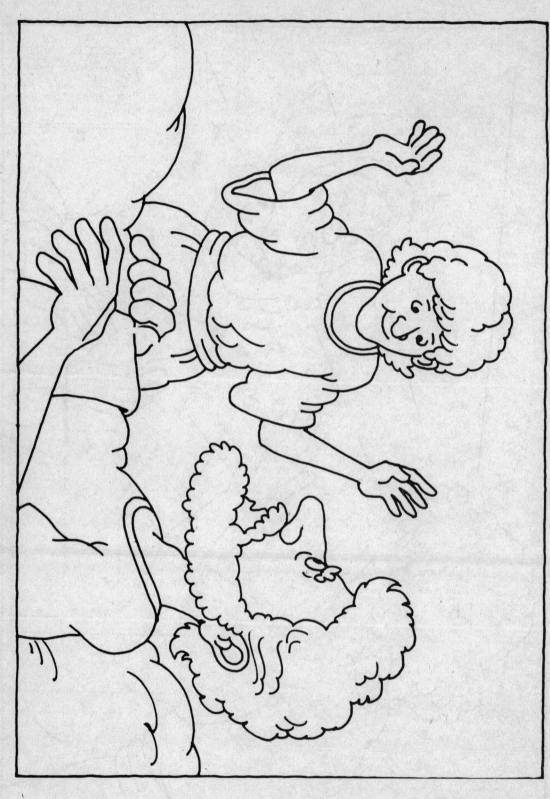

Mary was engaged to marry Joseph, so the angel went to see him, too. The angel told Joseph that Mary was going to have a baby who would be the son of God. The angel said that Joseph should marry her and take care of baby Jesus.

Mary Visits Elizabeth

Luke 1:39-45

With your pencil, help Mary find the way to Elizabeth's house.

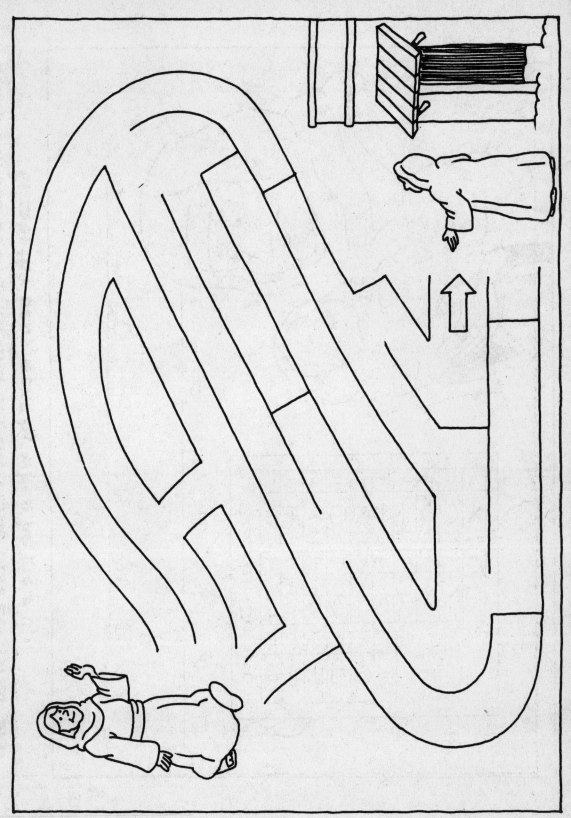

Mary was very excited about having a baby. She went to visit Elizabeth and they talked about their babies. Mary stayed with Elizabeth for about three months.

ELIZABETH AND ZECHARIAH'S BABY IS BORN

Break the secret code to find out the name that Zechariah and Elizabeth's baby went by when he grew up.

Luke 1:57–66

Secret Code			
a △	k ◁	u ▣	
b +	l ▽	v ◇	
c ▣	m ✦	w ▥	
d ○	n ↑	x ◻	
e ◯	o ◁	y ⊘	
f ▢	p ✕	z ▯	
g ▭	q ⊐		
h ◇	r ◁		
i ◖	s △		
j ✳	t ▤		

Elizabeth had a baby boy, just like the angel said she would. Zechariah and Elizabeth's relatives had opinions about what the baby's name should be. Most thought he should be called Zechariah or some other name that was in their family. But Elizabeth told them that the angel said what the baby should be named.

JOHN'S LIFE WORK

Luke 3:1-20

Color this picture of John.

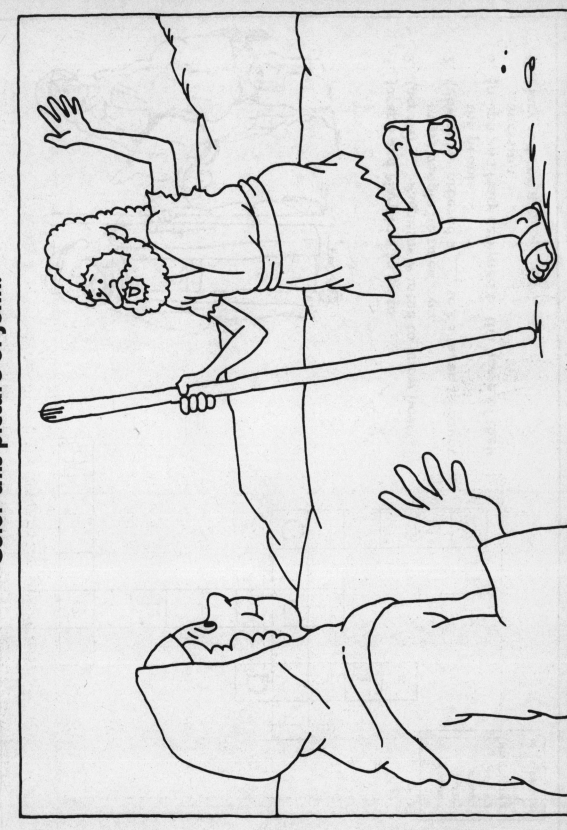

John's life work was to tell people that someone special would soon be coming. He was telling people that the Son of God was coming.

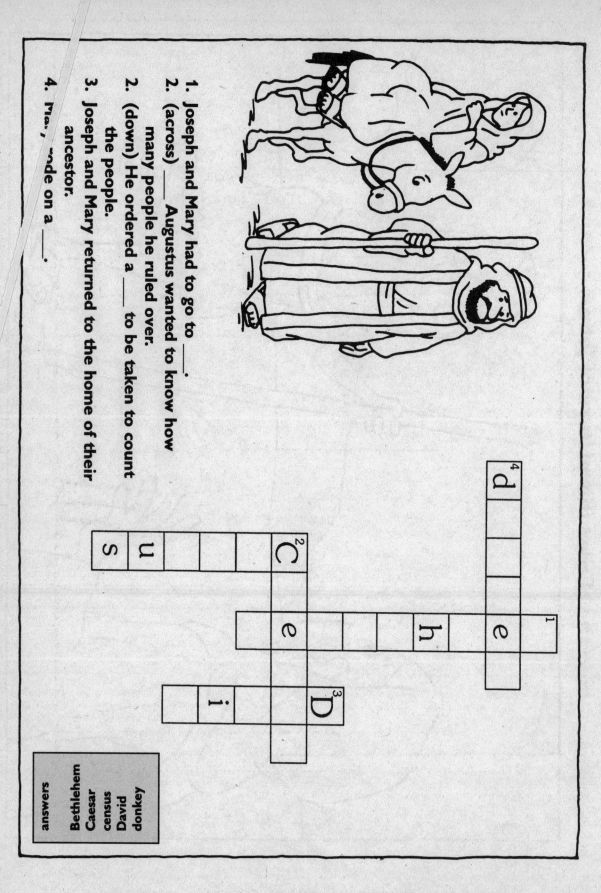

1. Joseph and Mary had to go to ____.
2. (across) ____ Augustus wanted to know how many people he ruled over.
2. (down) He ordered a ____ to be taken to count the people.
3. Joseph and Mary returned to the home of their ancestor.
4. Mary rode on a ____.

answers

Bethlehem
Caesar
census
David
donkey

It was nearly time for Mary's baby to be born, but she and Joseph had to take a trip. They had to go to Bethlehem to be counted in a census. Their ancestor, King David, was from Bethlehem.

FULL HOUSE

Luke 2:1-7

Find the shapes in the key box in the picture.

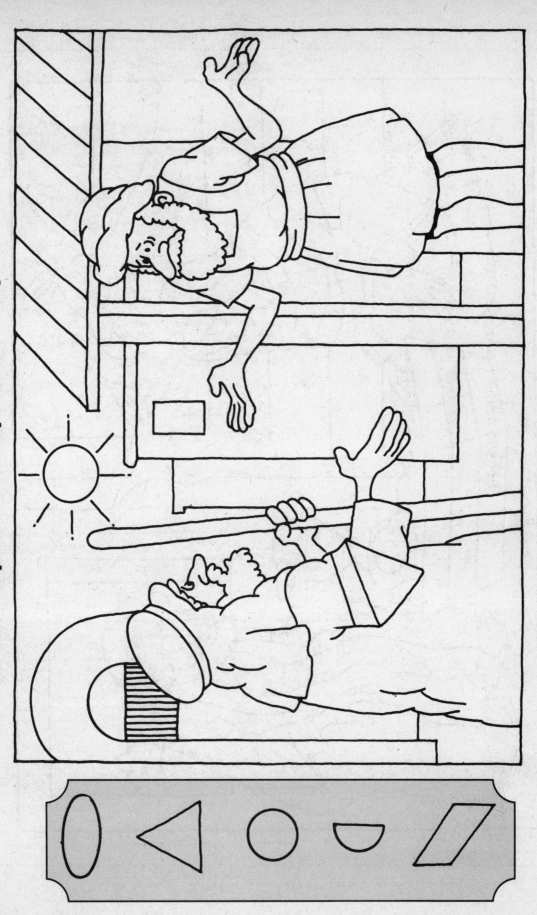

Bethlehem was crowded with people who were in town to be counted in the census. Mary and Joseph couldn't find any-place to stay. Joseph looked everywhere and even though Mary's baby was ready to be born, they could not find a room.

A SPECIAL BIRTH

Color this picture.

Finally one innkeeper offered his stable to Joseph and Mary. So they settled in there for the night. That special night, baby Jesus was born. Mary wrapped him in strips of cloth and laid him in the animals' feed trough to sleep.

AN ANGEL CHORUS

Luke 2:8–20

These two pictures may look the same, but there are six things different in the second picture. Find and circle those differences.

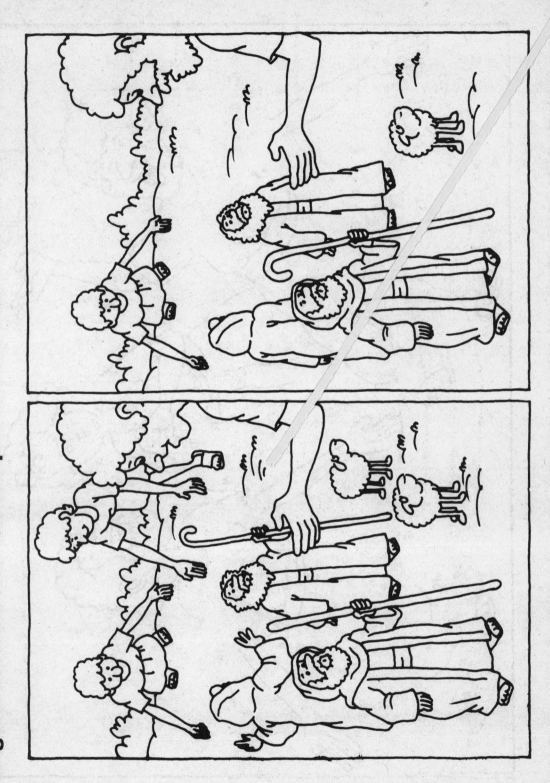

Some shepherds were watching their sheep on the hills outside Bethlehem. Suddenly the dark sky glowed bright, with an angel. The angel told the shepherds that a special baby had been born that night in Bethlehem.

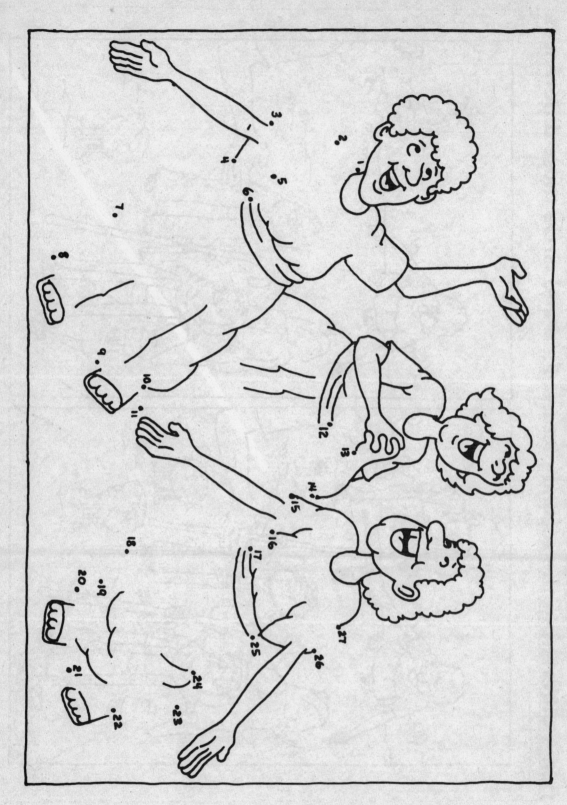

After the angel told the shepherds about Jesus' birth, a whole choir of angels appeared in the sky. They sang, "Glory to God in the highest, and on earth peace, goodwill toward men."

The Shepherds Hurry to Bethlehem

Luke 2:13–20

Help the shepherds find the stable so they can see the new baby.

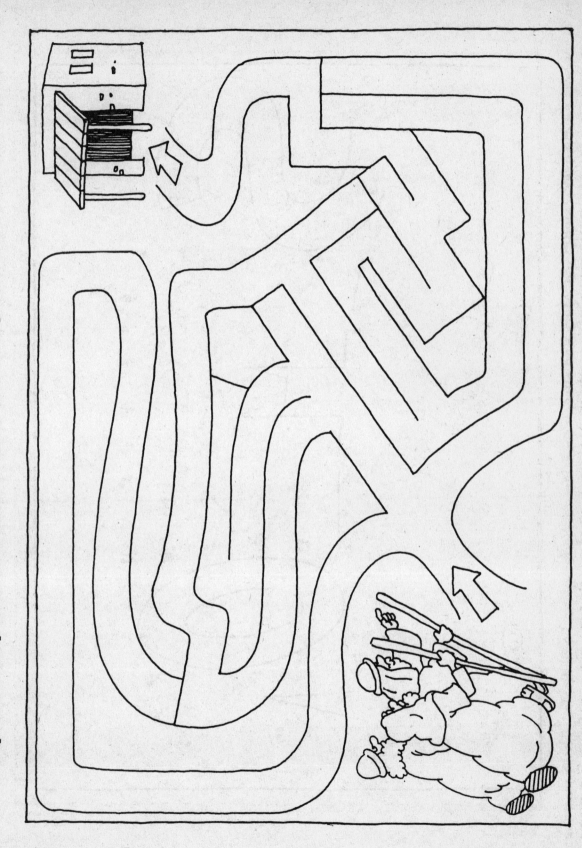

After the angels sang they disappeared. Then the shepherds hurried to Bethlehem to see the new baby.

THE DEDICATION OF JESUS

Luke 2:21–40

Connect the dots to spell a name.

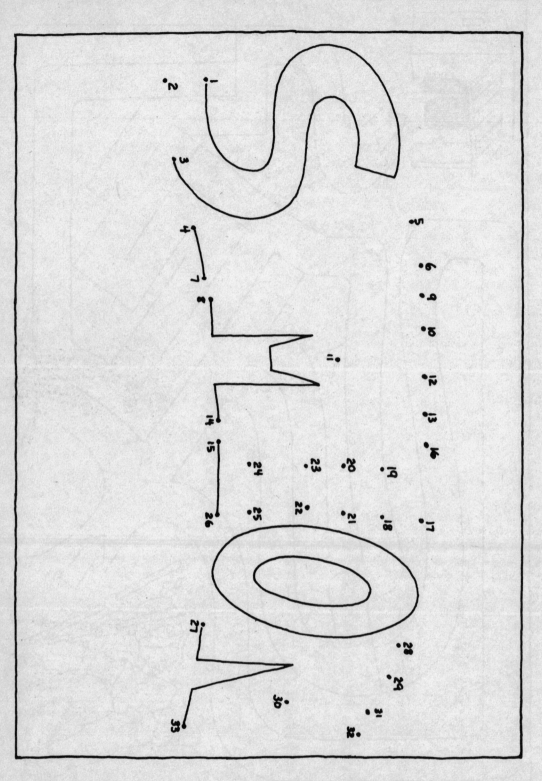

When Jesus was a little over a month old, Mary and Joseph took him to the temple to be dedicated. There was a man in the temple that day who loved God very much. In fact, God had promised the man that he wouldn't die until he had seen the Messiah. When the man saw baby Jesus, he said, "Now, I can die!"

THE BIRTH OF JESUS

Matthew 2:1, 2; Luke 2:1–16

Read the story of Jesus' birth in Luke 2:1-16 and Matthew 2:1, 2 and match the correct picture to the statement.

_____ Announced the birth of Jesus

_____ Baby Jesus was laid in this

_____ Led the wise men to Jesus

_____ Wise men traveled on this

_____ They came right away to see Jesus

1.

2.

3.

4.

5.

Sweet Old Anna

Luke 2:36-40

Color this picture.

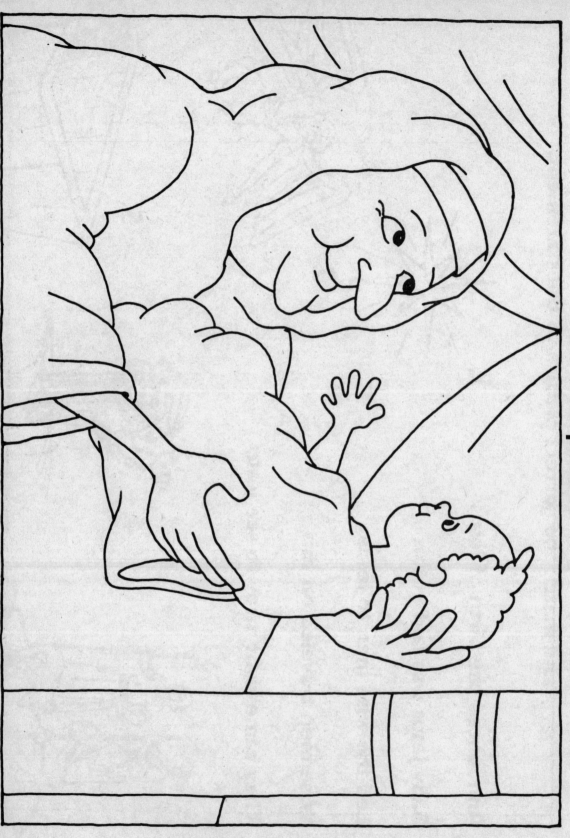

An old woman named Anna was also in the temple the day that Jesus was dedicated. When she saw baby Jesus she praised God. She told everyone she saw that the Messiah had been born.

The Wise Men See a Star

Matthew 2:1-6

Trace over the dotted line to finish this picture.

At about the same time that Jesus was born some wise men in a country far away from Bethlehem saw a new star in the sky. They believed that the star meant that the Messiah had been born.

THE WISE MEN FIND JESUS

Matthew 2:9-12

Look for items shown in the key box in the picture below. When you find them, circle them.

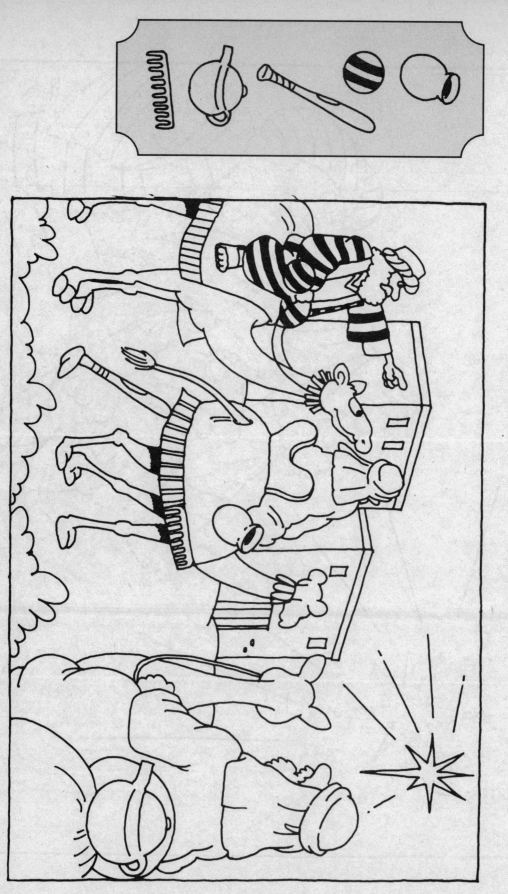

The wise men knew the Scriptures that spoke of a Messiah being born. They wanted to see the special baby so they began the long journey to find Jesus. The star led them all the way to Bethlehem.

WISE MEN FOLLOW A STAR

Matthew 2:9

The wise men are following the star to baby Jesus. Help them find their way.

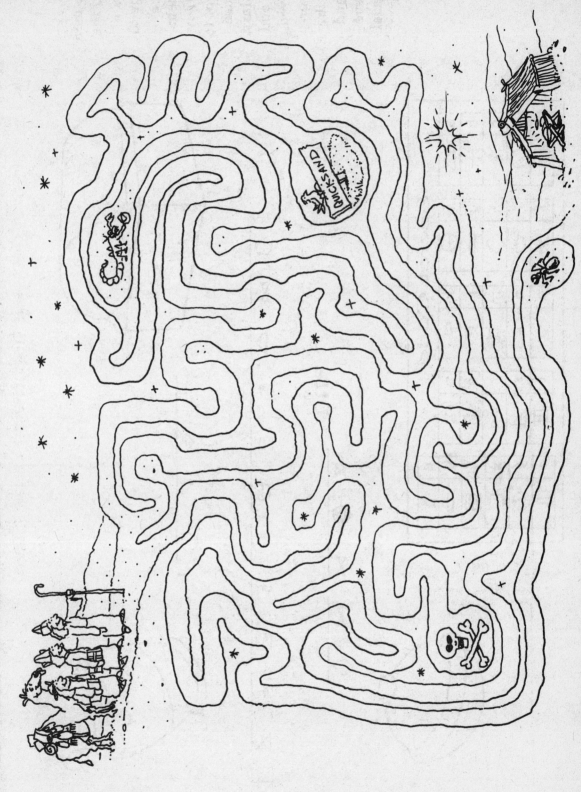

The wise men followed a special star that led them all the way to baby Jesus.

SPECIAL GIFTS FOR A SPECIAL CHILD

Matthew 2:10-11

Break the secret code to find out what gifts the wise men brought to young Jesus.

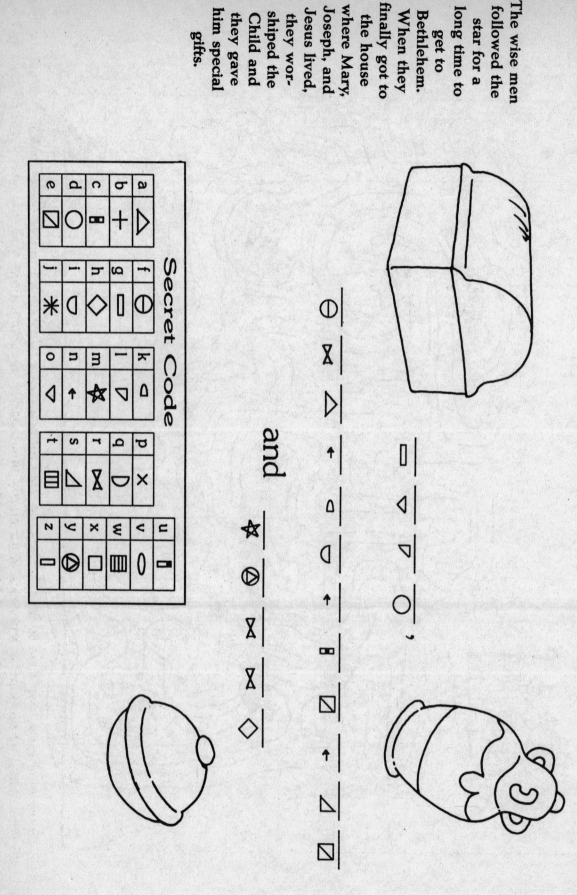

The wise men followed the star for a long time to get to Bethlehem. When they finally got to the house where Mary, Joseph, and Jesus lived, they worshiped the Child and they gave him special gifts.

Secret Code

a △	b +	c ▯	d ○	e ◻
f ⊖	g ▭	h ◇	i ⌓	j ✳
k ◁	l ▽	m ☆	n ↑	o ◁
p ✕	q ◸	r ⋈	s △	t ▥
u ▯	v ◯	w ▤	x ◻	y ⊘	z ▯

Jealous King Herod

Matthew 2:13–18

Connect the dots to complete this picture.

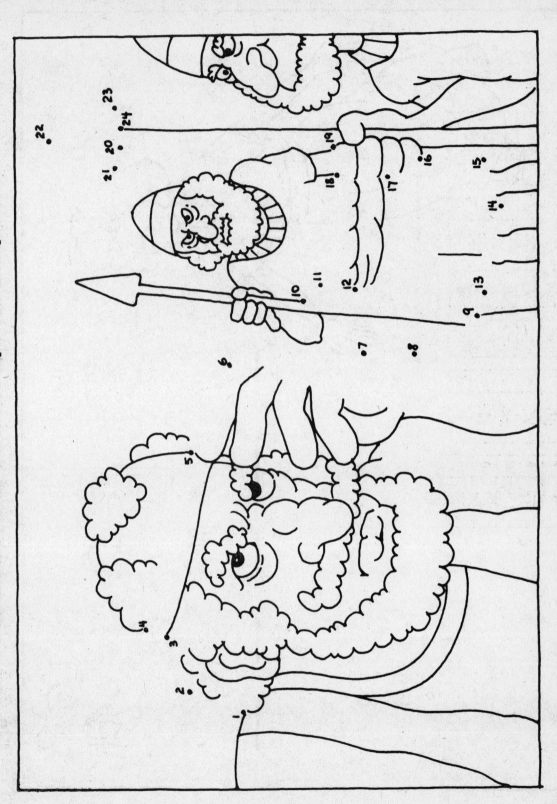

The wise men traveled for a long time to find Jesus. One time they stopped and asked King Herod if he knew anything about the child who would be the king of the Jews. King Herod immediately became jealous that this boy might take away his kingdom. He asked the wise men to let him know when they found the boy. He secretly began to plan to kill Jesus.

A SPECIAL MESSAGE FOR JOSEPH

Matthew 2:13

Unscramble this word to find out who told Joseph the message.

g l n e a

_ _ _ _ _

King Herod commanded that all boys who were two years old or younger should be killed. He thought this was the best way to get rid of Jesus. King Herod didn't know that Joseph had been warned to take Jesus out of the country.

HIDING IN EGYPT

Matthew 2:14–15

Find the shapes shown in the key box in the picture. Circle them.

An angel came to Joseph during the night and told him to take Mary and Jesus to Egypt.

JESUS IS BORN

Read Luke 2:1-7 and use the clues in the word box to work the crossword puzzle.

Down

1. Mary and Joseph were traveling because of a ___.
2. Bethlehem is called the "City of ___."
4. His mother put Jesus in a ___.
5. Mary's husband and Jesus' father on earth was ___.
8. The name of the city where Jesus was born was ___.

Across

3. ___ told the shepherds about Jesus.
6. There was no room in the ___.
7. A ___ led the wise men to Jesus.
9. Wise men brought ___ to Jesus.
10. Jesus was born in a ___.
11. ___ followed the star.

THE ANGEL SAYS, "ALL CLEAR!"

Matthew 2:19–23

Trace over the dotted lines to finish the picture.

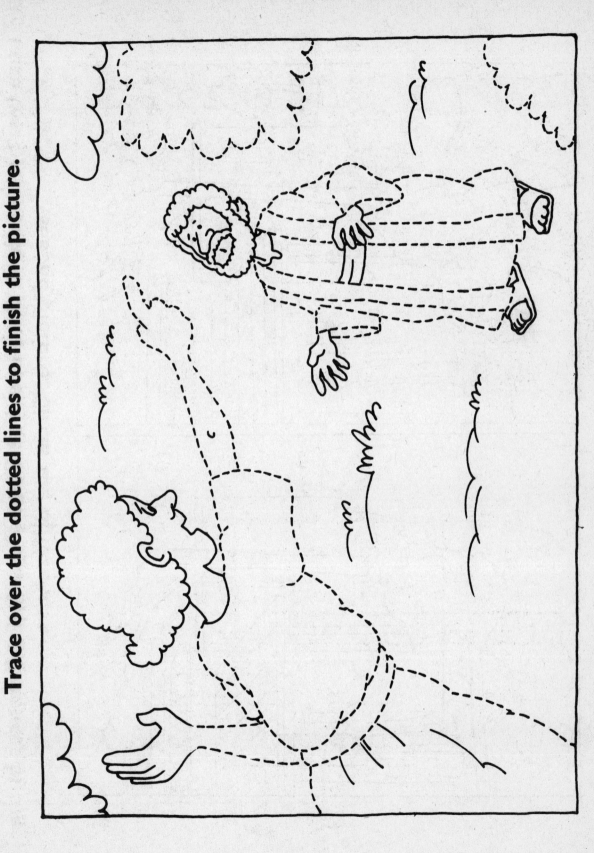

After a while King Herod died. Then the angel came back to Joseph and told him that it was safe to take Jesus back home.

GOING HOME TO NAZARETH

Matthew 2:21-23

These two pictures look the same, but there are seven differences in the second picture. Circle the differences.

Joseph was happy to finally be able to take his family back to his hometown, Nazareth. He hadn't been there for a long, long time.

LEARNING TO BE A CARPENTER

Luke 2:40

Color this picture.

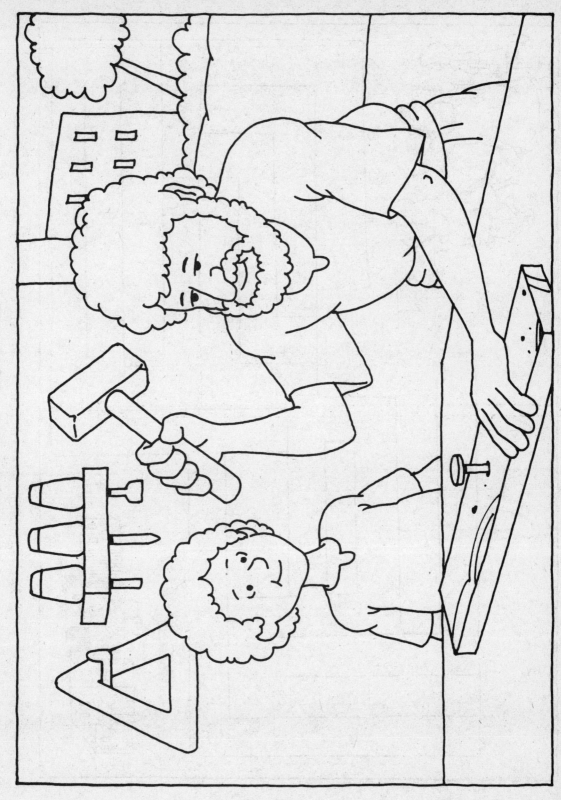

As soon as Mary and Joseph got settled in Nazareth, Joseph had to start earning money. He opened his carpenter shop and began teaching Jesus how to be a carpenter.

JESUS FIRST TRIP TO JERUSALEM

Luke 2:41-52

Joseph, Mary, and Jesus want to go to Jerusalem. Can you help them find the way?

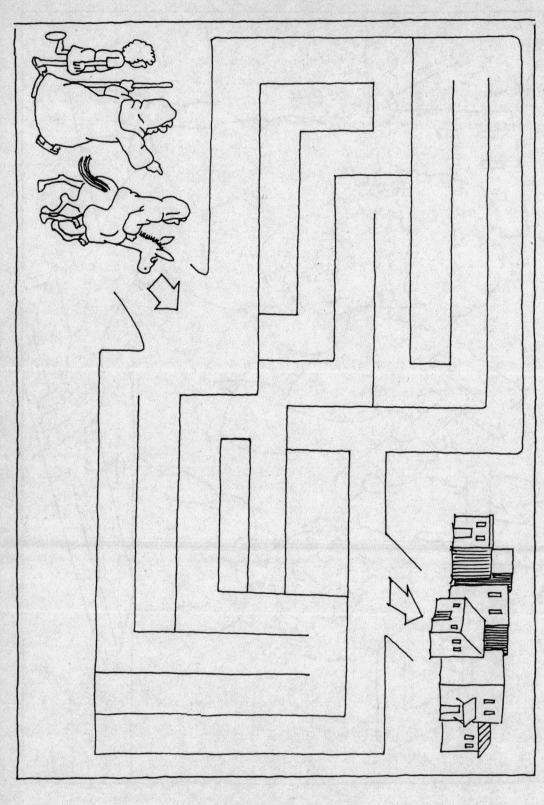

When Jesus was twelve years old he went to Jerusalem with his parents to celebrate the Passover Feast. Mary and Joseph went every year, but this was the first time Jesus was old enough to go along.

Jesus Stays Behind

Luke 2:41-52

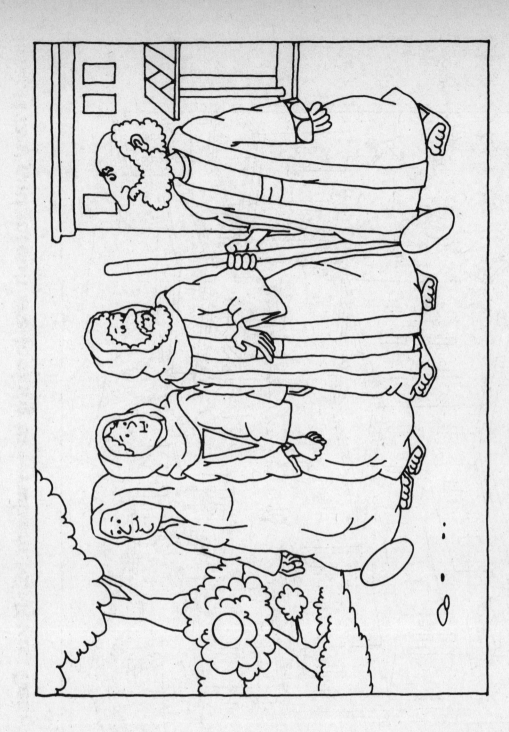

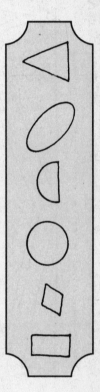

Find the shapes in the key box in the picture below.

After the Passover celebration, Mary and Joseph began the trip home. They were walking with many of their friends and relatives. Mary and Joseph noticed that Jesus wasn't with them but they thought he was probably walking with some of his friends. However, they soon realized that Jesus had been left behind in Jerusalem.

LOOKING FOR JESUS

Luke 2:41-52

Mary and Joseph are looking everywhere for Jesus. Can you find him?

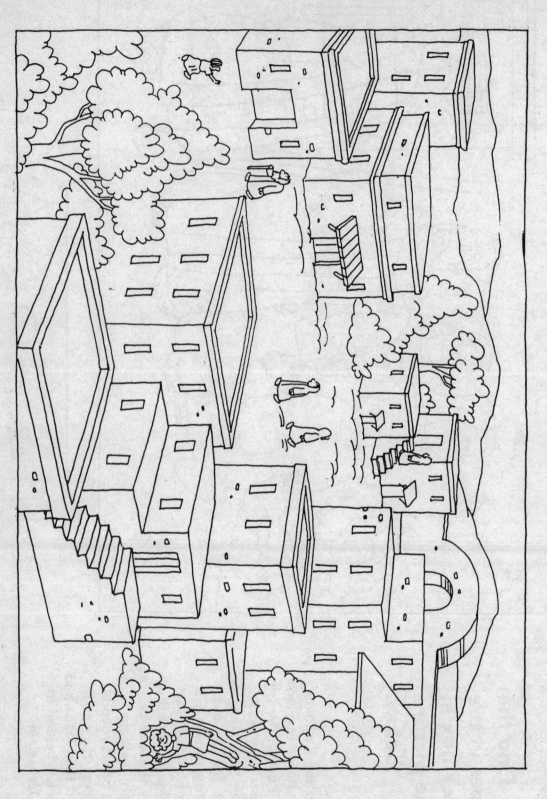

Mary and Joseph rushed back to Jerusalem. They looked everywhere for Jesus. They searched throughout the city for three days.

Jesus Is Found

Luke 2:41–52

Trace over the letters to spell the name of the place where Jesus was found.

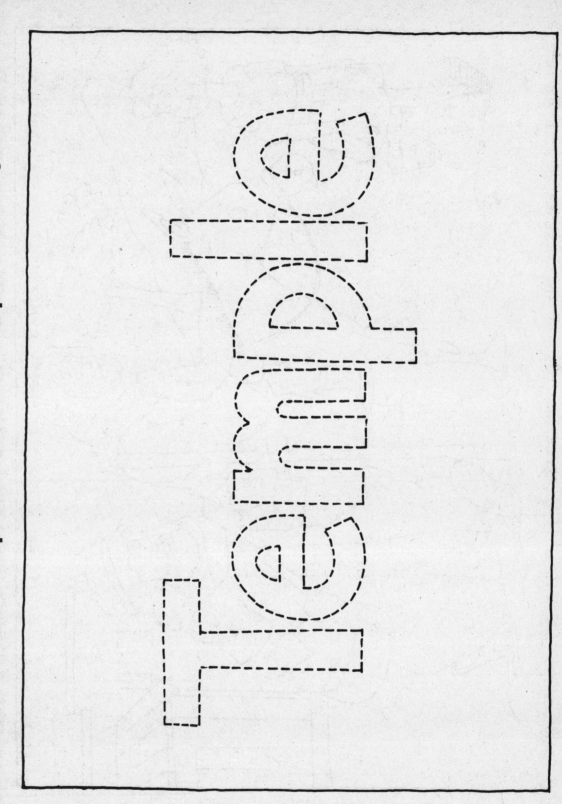

Finally, Mary and Joseph found Jesus. They were surprised to find him in the temple talking to the teachers. Everyone who heard him was amazed at how well he understood the teachings of God.

JESUS GOES HOME

Luke 2:41-52

Color this picture.

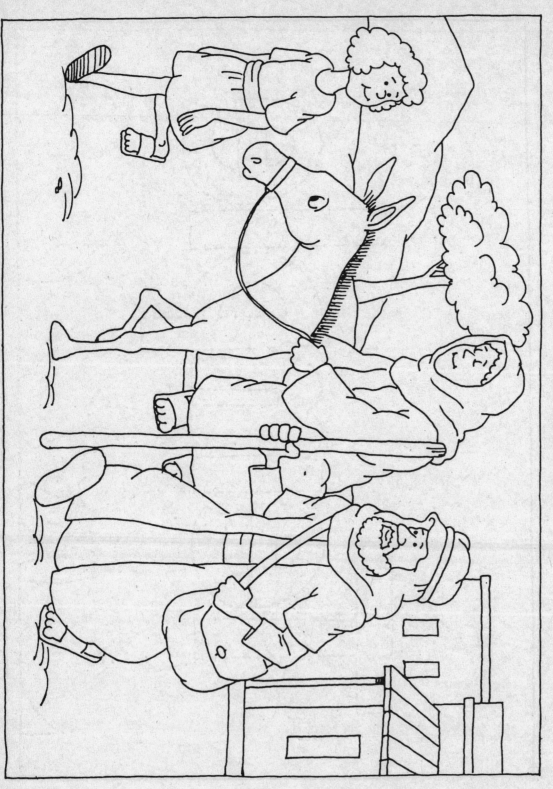

Mary and Joseph found Jesus talking to people in the temple. He was happy to go home with his parents. He always obeyed his parents. Jesus kept growing taller and stronger. Everyone who knew him liked him.

Jesus Goes to a Wedding

John 2:1–11

Color this picture.

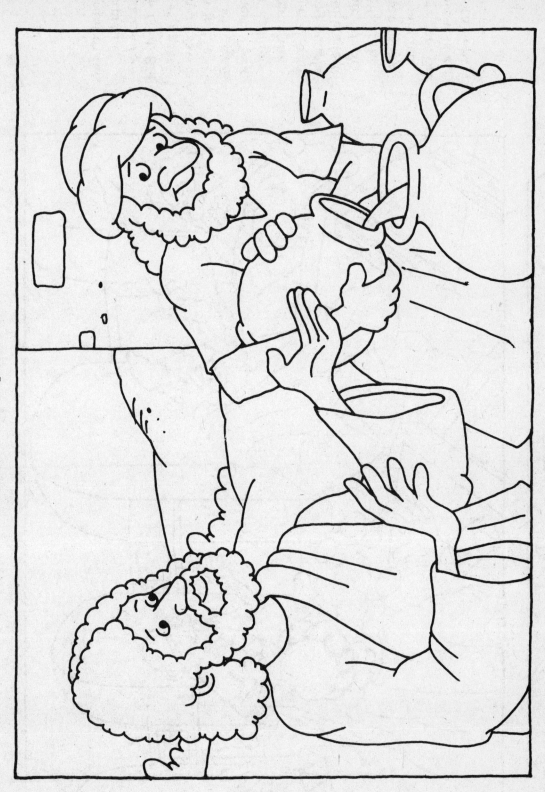

One time Jesus and his friends were at a wedding in Cana. Jesus' mother was there, also. The host ran out of the wine he was serving the wedding guests. Mary asked Jesus to help the man. So Jesus did his first miracle. He turned plain old water into wine.

JESUS CLEANS UP THE TEMPLE

John 2:12-17

Circle the items in the key box in the big picture.

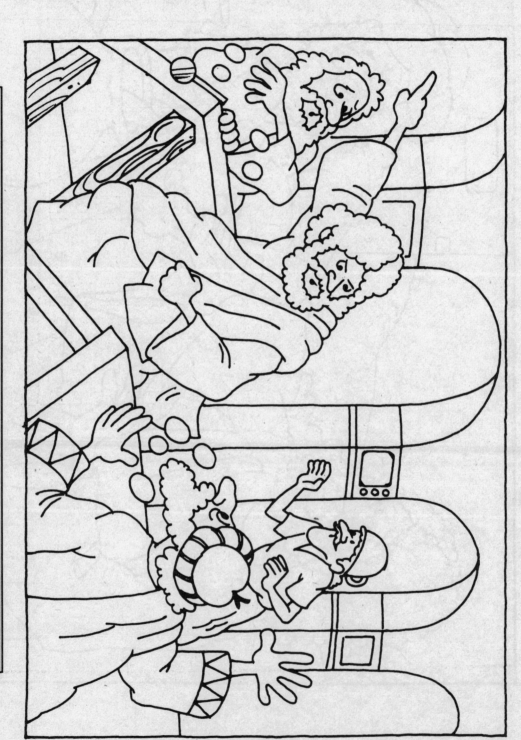

Jesus went to the temple in Jerusalem to worship God. But he was upset when he saw men in the temple who were dishonest. They were selling things in the temple and were cheating people who had come to worship. Jesus chased all the bad men away. He reminded everyone that the temple was a place to pray.

An Eager Student

John 3:1-21

Figure out this secret code to see who wanted to learn more about God.

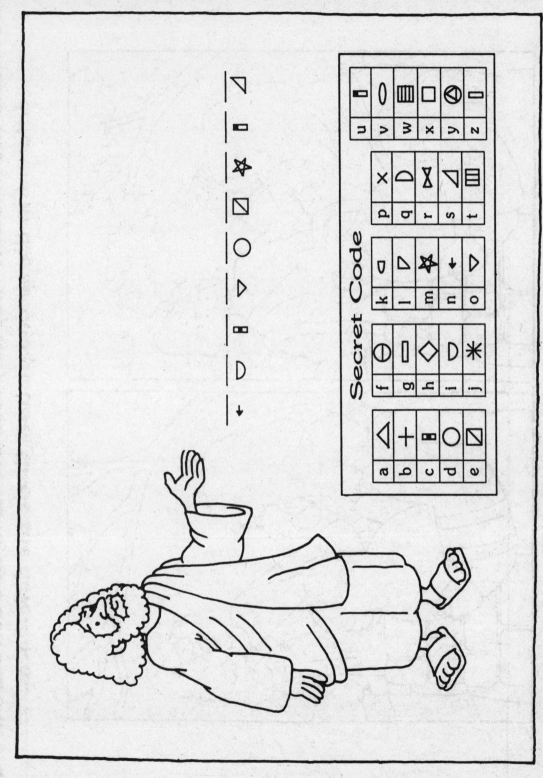

Secret Code

a	◁	f	⊖	k	◁	p	✕	u	▯
b	✛	g	▭	l	▱	q	◻	v	◊
c	▣	h	◇	m	✦	r	✕	w	☰
d	◯	i	◁	n	↓	s	◁	x	◻
e	◺	j	✳	o	▷	t	☰	y	⊘
								z	▭

One night a man secretly came to see Jesus. He wanted to know more about God. Jesus told the man how he could know God.

THE WOMAN AT THE WELL

John 4:1-26

Look at these two pictures. They may look the same, but there are five things different in the second picture. Circle the differences.

Jesus met a woman at a well. He asked her for a drink of water. She was surprised when he told her all about her. She had never seen him before but he knew all about her. The woman ran back to town shouting that she had met the Messiah.

Jesus Heals a Little Boy

John 4:43-54

The shapes in the box are hidden in the picture. Can you find them?

One time a royal official came to ask for Jesus' help. The man's son was very sick and he believed that Jesus could make the boy well. The man wanted Jesus to come to his house. But Jesus said, "You can go home. Your son is well." The man believed Jesus and went home to find that his son was fine!

A SPECIAL TIME FOR PETER

Matthew 14:22-36

Use every seventh letter starting from the top left and going left to right to find out what special thing Peter did. The first letter is circled for you.

```
M  E  W  S  R  A  Ⓦ  T
H  Y  N  J  H  A  J  M
K  I  L  O  L  B  G  V
F  C  D  K  S  A  Z  Q
W  E  E  K  I  J  U  Y
H  D  T  R  F  D  E  W
O  A  Q  N  Z  X  C  V  N
G  N  H  M  J  K  W  G
Y  J  U  N  I  A  O  L
P  T  F  G  T  F  Y  G
E  D  S  E  W  Q  A  Z
S  X  R  Z  C  F  V  G
```

___   ___   ___   ___   ___   ___

Peter and the disciples were in a boat, crossing the lake late one night. They were very surprised to look out and see Jesus walking toward them on top of the water! Then Jesus helped Peter do something that was very special.

A FISHING MIRACLE

John 21:1–14

Color this picture.

Jesus was teaching some people beside a big lake. There were some fishermen out in their boats. They had been fishing all night, but hadn't caught anything. Jesus told them to put their nets in the water and try again. When they did, they caught so many fish that they couldn't pull the nets in.

JESUS HEALS A WOMAN

Matthew 8:14-16; Mark 1:29-34

Trace these letters to write the name of Jesus' friend.

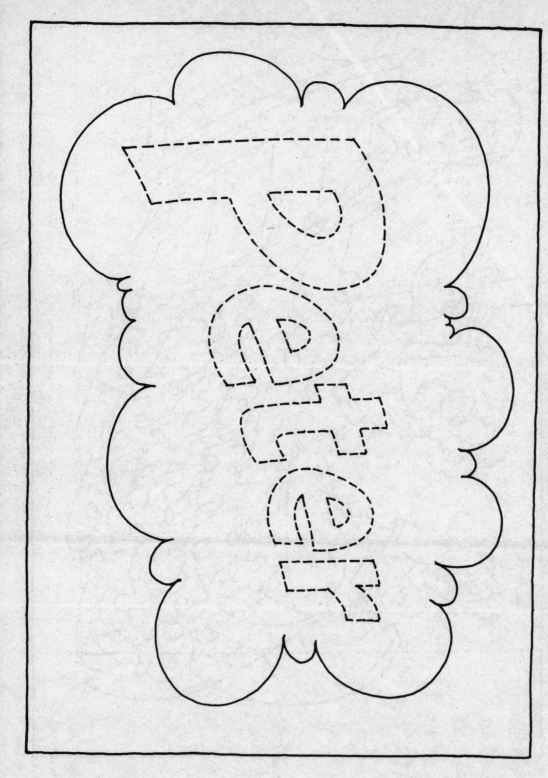

Jesus was visiting his friend, Peter. Peter's mother-in-law was very sick. Everyone was worried about her because her fever was so high. Jesus went to the woman's bedside and told the fever to go away. The woman got up right away.

She was healed!

Healings In Galilee

Matthew 8:17

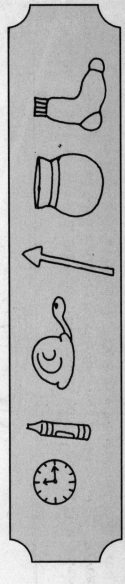

Circle the items in the box in the picture.

Jesus traveled all around Galilee teaching people about God. Many people brought their sick friends and family members to Jesus because they believed Jesus could heal them.

THE POOL OF BETHESDA

John 5:1-15

Color this picture.

People believed that the water in the Pool of Bethesda could heal the first person to get in it after the water was stirred up. One man had been trying to be the first one in the pool for 38 years but he was always too slow. When Jesus said to the man, "Pick up your mat and walk!" the man was healed.

A Handy Healing

Mark 3:1–6

Connect the dots to finish the picture.

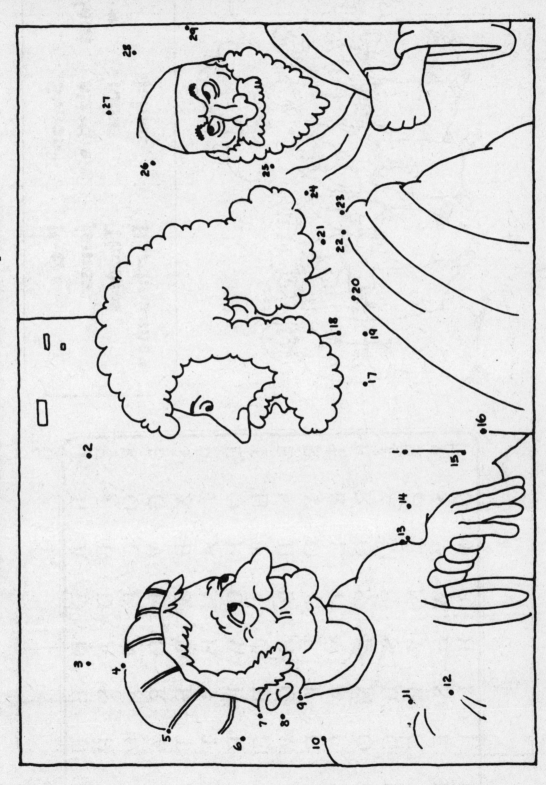

One time Jesus was praying in the synagogue and he saw a man who had a crippled hand. Jesus felt bad for the man so he healed his hand. This happened on the Sabbath when no work was supposed to be done. So the Pharisees accused Jesus of breaking the law.

Matthew 10

Find and circle the names in the box in the puzzle below.

Philip	Simon	Peter
Thaddeus	Matthew	James
Andrew	Judas	Thomas
John	James	Bartholomew

```
T H A D D E U S R
E J U D A S H Y J
K O L P N J M M N
B G V F D R A E W
S X B S R F T J G
P J A M E S T H M
E O R O W P E H T
T H T S Q D E X H
R Y O Y F F H Y O
E N H B H G W F O
T R L T Y P I H M
F R O S I M O N S
R H E N V B H A T
J A M E S H G Y M
R S W E S B G F O
W S W P H E V X T
F U Y P H I L I P
```

Jesus chose twelve men to be his special friends or disciples. They traveled everywhere with Jesus, listening to him teach, and seeing him do wonderful miracles.

JESUS TEACHES BY THE SEA

Matthew 3:7–12

Look at the items in the box. Find and circle them in the picture.

Everywhere Jesus went people followed along. They wanted to hear his teachings and see the miracles he did.

Twelve Special Friends

Mark 3:13-19

Use the names in the box to work this crossword puzzle. These are the men Jesus called to be his disciples.

Peter	James
John	Andrew
Philip	Bartholomew
Matthew	Thomas
James	Thaddaeus
Simon	Judas

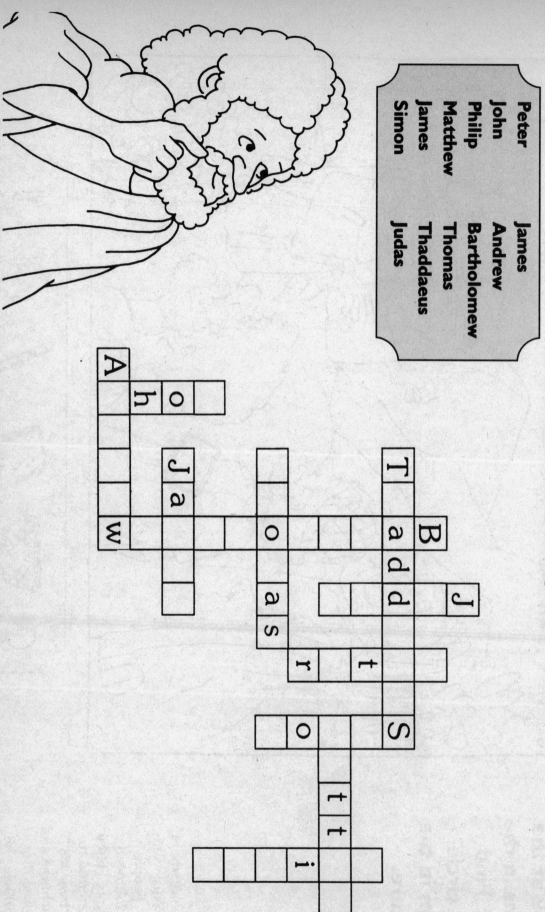

Jesus chose twelve men to be his special friends. They left their jobs and spent their time with him.

Matthew's Job

Acts 1:12-26

Cross out all of the D, F, B, S, H, I and G's to see what Matthew's job was before he followed Jesus. Write your answer on the lines.

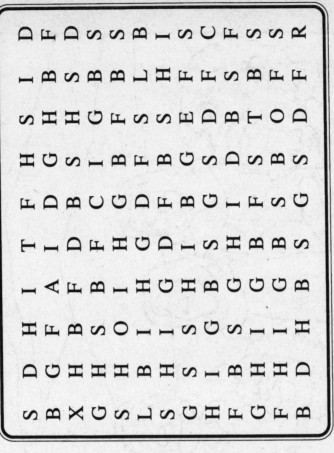

```
S D H I T F H S I D
B G F A I D G H B F
X H B F D B S H S D
G H S B F C I G B S
S H O I H G B F B S
L B I H O F D F L B
S H I G H D F B S H I
G S S H I B G E F S
H I G B S G S D F C
F B S G I H I D B S
G H I G B F B F S T
F H I G B S B O F S
B D H B S G S D F R
```

- - - - - - - - - - -

Matthew was one of Jesus' disciples. Before Jesus called him to be a follower, Matthew had a very unpopular position.

THE SERMON ON THE MOUNT

Matthew 5–7

Color this picture.

One time Jesus went up on a mountain. Many people followed him. Jesus taught the people many things about God and how to live for him.

THE CENTURION'S SERVANT

Matthew 8:5–13

Find the five differences in these two pictures.

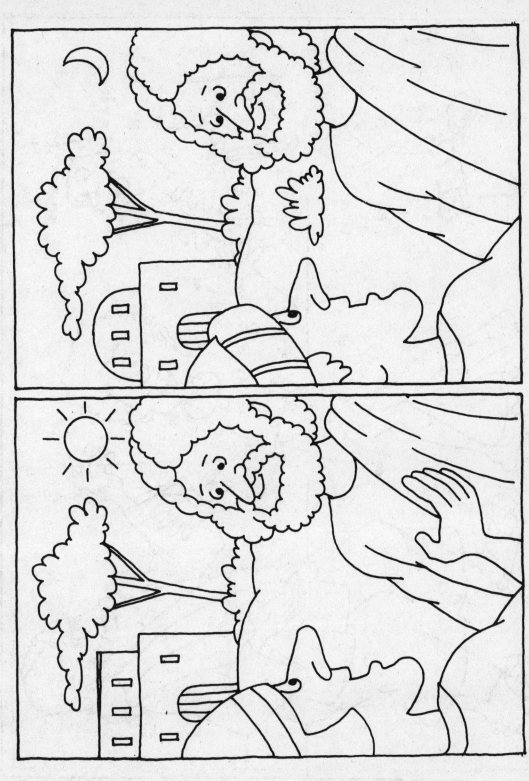

A Roman army officer, called a centurion, came to Jesus and said, "My servant is paralyzed." Jesus started to go to the centurion's house to heal the servant, but the man said, "You don't have to come. You can just say the words and my servant will be healed." Jesus was amazed at the man's faith, so he spoke the words and the servant was healed.

Jesus saw a heartbroken mother. Her husband was dead and now her only son had died. Jesus felt sorry for the mother so he went to the dead boy and said, "Get up!" The boy did get up. He was alive again!

Jesus Stops a Storm

Mark 4:35–41

Trace over the dotted lines to finish this picture.

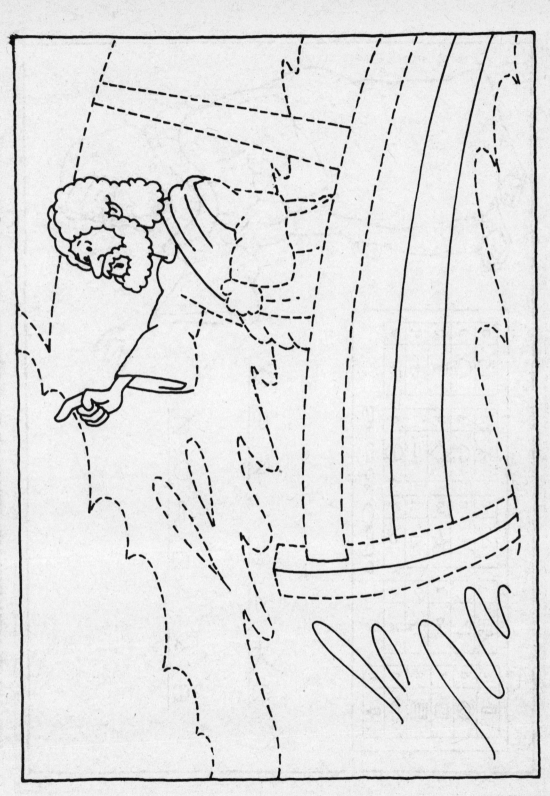

Jesus and his disciples were in a boat crossing the sea. Jesus was very tired so he fell asleep. Suddenly a big storm blew up on the sea. The disciples were afraid they were going to die so they woke Jesus. He stood up and told the wind to be quiet. The storm stopped! Then the disciples knew that Jesus is the Son of God.

A Woman with Great Faith

Matthew 9:20-26

Break the secret code to figure out what the woman touched.

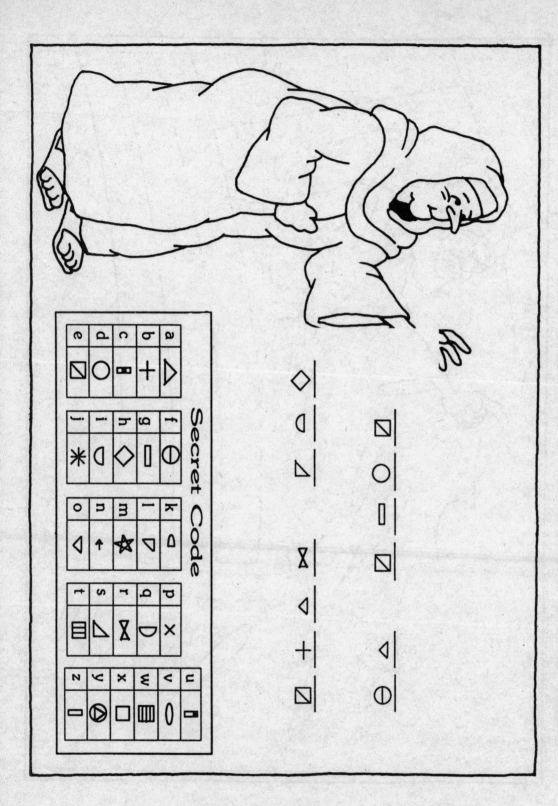

Secret Code

a	△
b	+
c	☰
d	○
e	▢

f	⊖
g	▢
h	◇
i	◖
j	✳

k	◁
l	▽
m	☆
n	↑
o	◁

p	✕
q	◫
r	▷
s	△
t	⊞

u	▮
v	◯
w	⊟
x	▢
y	◉
z	▯

Jesus was walking down the street, surrounded by people. Suddenly he stopped and said, "Who touched me?" He knew someone had touched him because he felt power leave him. A woman who had been sick for years and years had touched his robe because she believed that would make her well.

Jairus' Daughter

Mark 5:22-43

Color this picture.

Jairus asked Jesus to help his sick daughter, but it was too late, the little girl was dead. Jairus was so sad! Then Jesus said, "Wait a minute. Don't cry, your daughter is just asleep, she's not dead." Some people laughed at Jesus, but he went to the girl and said, "Get up!" and she did! Then Jesus told her parents to get her some food.

JESUS SENDS THE DISCIPLES OUT

Matthew 10

Help the disciples get to another town so they can tell more people about Jesus.

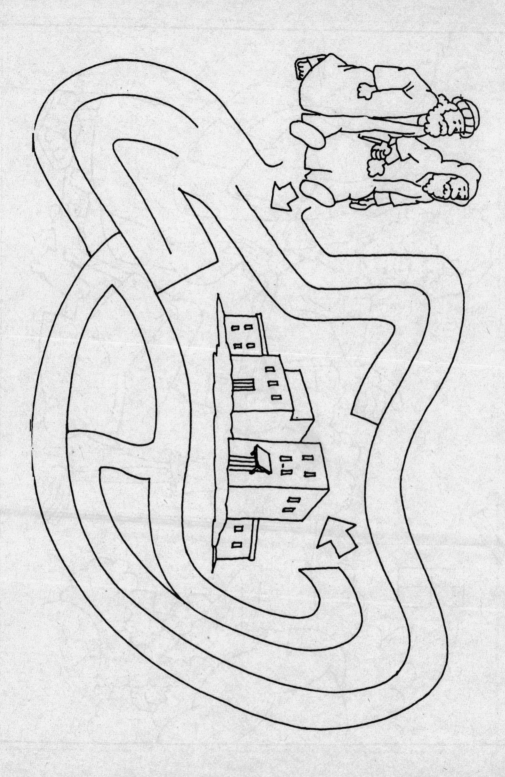

Jesus knew that he wouldn't be on earth much longer. So he taught his disciples what they needed to know about God. He told them to teach people everywhere about God. He gave them the power to heal people, too. Then Jesus sent them out in groups of two to do his work.

A MIRACLE MEAL

John 6:1–15

Use the clues to finish the crossword.

1. Who did the lunch belong to?
2. How much bread was in the lunch?
3. What else was in the lunch?
4. Jesus fed more than ____ people.
5. How many baskets of food were left over?

1 = Boy
2 = Five Loaves
3 = Two Fish
4 = Five Thousand
5 = Twelve

More than 5,000 people were listening to Jesus teach. When dinnertime came a little boy gave Jesus his lunch of five loaves of bread and two fish. Jesus blessed the food and broke it into pieces. Everyone there had all the food they wanted to eat—and there were twelve baskets of leftovers!

Find and circle the items in the box in the picture of Jesus.

JESUS WALKS ON THE WATER

John 6:16-24

Late one night Jesus' disciples were crossing the lake. The wind was blowing and the waves were pretty big. Suddenly they saw someone walking on top of the water toward them. It was Jesus!

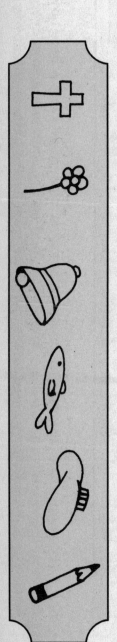

THE TRANSFIGURATION

Mark 9:2-13

Color this picture.

Jesus took three of his closest friends up to the top of a mountain. They watched while Jesus prayed. As he was praying, Jesus began to glow. Moses and Elijah suddenly appeared and talked with Jesus. This was called the Transfiguration.

TWO SPECIAL FRIENDS

Cross out every other letter. The remaining letters will spell the names of two of Jesus' special friends.

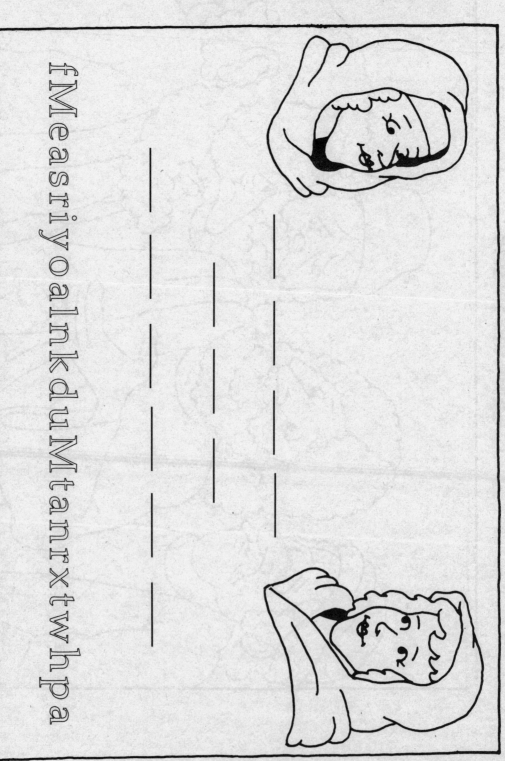

fMeasriyoalnkduMtanrxtwhpa

_____ _____ _____

Jesus went to Bethany to visit two of his special friends. The two sisters were very happy to see Jesus. One sat and talked to him while the other worked hard preparing dinner. Martha, the worker, thought her sister, Mary, should help her. But Jesus explained that it was really more important to spend time with him.

JESUS CRIES

Matthew 23:37-39

Color this picture.

Jesus was very sad because he knew that many people in Jerusalem didn't love God. He was so sad that he cried for the people of Jerusalem.

LAZARUS

John 11:1-44

Connect the dots to finish this picture.

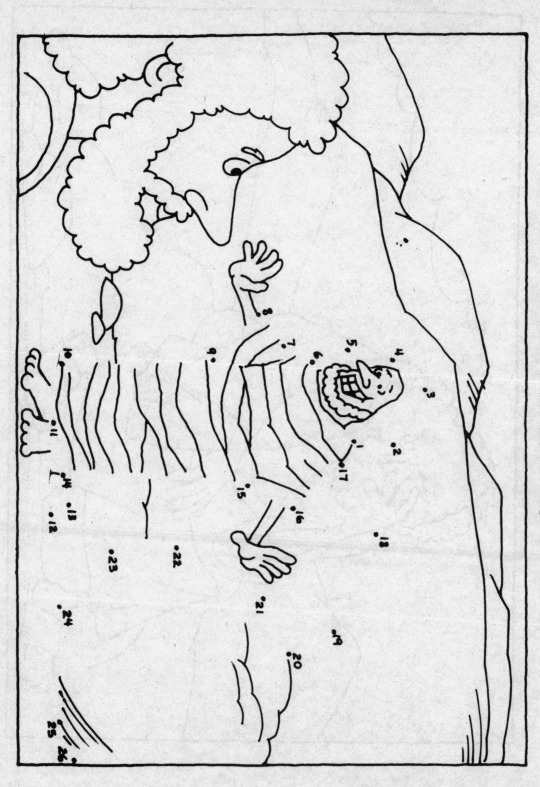

Mary, Martha, and Lazarus were close friends of Jesus. When Lazarus got very sick, his sisters sent for Jesus. But Jesus didn't go to Bethany right away. He waited until Lazarus was dead. Then he went to Bethany and told Mary and Martha to trust him. He went to the tomb and raised Lazarus from the dead.

A Special Woman

Acts 9:36–42

Use the first letter in each picture to find the name of this special woman. If you need help, look up Acts 9:36–42.

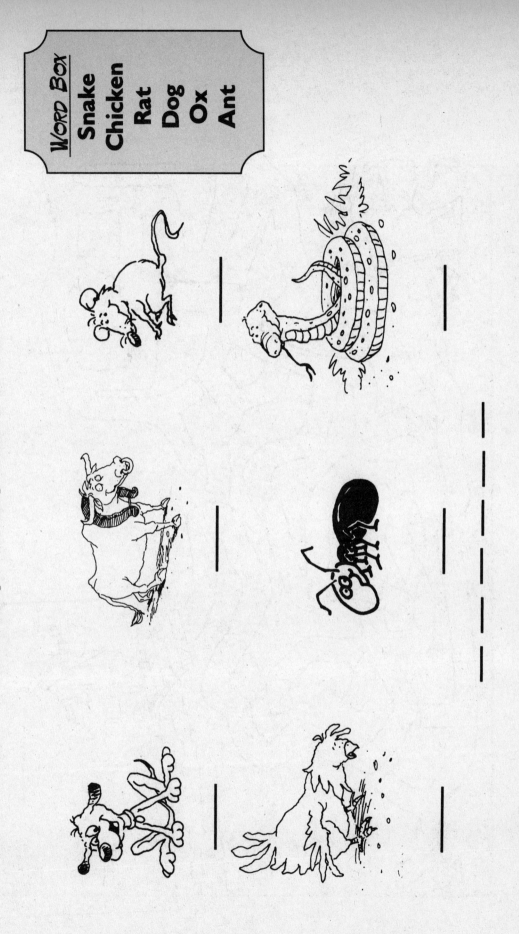

___   ___

_ _ _ _ _

___   ___

There was a woman who showed her love for Jesus by the things she did for her friends. She got sick and died, but God used Peter to bring her back to life.

A BRAND NEW LIFE

John 5:1-9

Help the man find his way to Jesus.

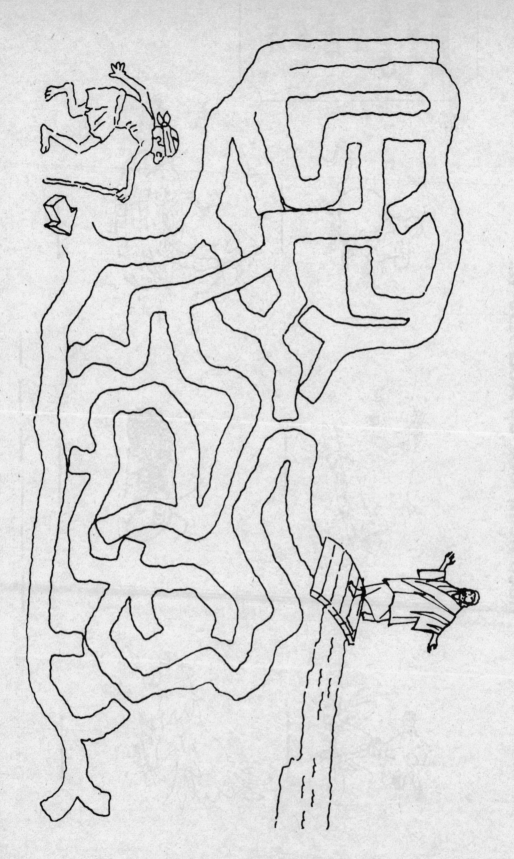

Jesus met a man who was crippled. He told the man to get up and walk. The man believed that Jesus is the Son of God, so he stood up and walked home. He was healed.

Down Through The Roof

Matthew 9:1–8; Mark 2:1–12

Help these men get their sick friend to Jesus.

Jesus was teaching at a house in Capernaum. Four men brought their sick friend to Jesus to be healed. But so many people were in the house that they couldn't get their friend inside. Finally they went up to the roof of the house, made a hole in the roof and lowered their friend down right in front of Jesus.

TEN HAPPY MEN

Luke 17:11-19

Figure out the secret code and see how many men remembered to thank Jesus.

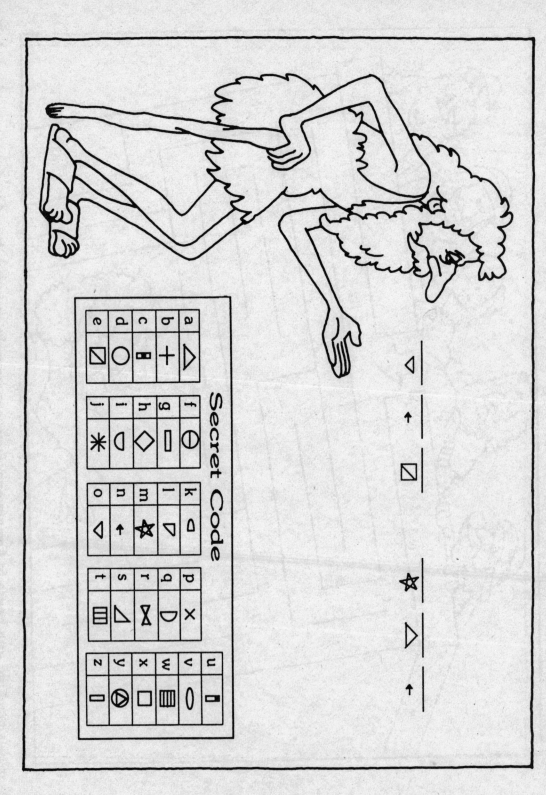

Secret Code

a	▷	f	⊕	k	◁	p	✕	u	▭
b	✚	g	▭	l	▽	q	◗	v	◯
c	⬛	h	◇	m	☆	r	⋈	w	☰
d	◯	i	◖	n	↑	s	△	x	▢
e	▱	j	✳	o	◁	t	▥	y	◉
								z	▯

Jesus was going to Jerusalem when he met ten men who had a terrible skin disease called leprosy. Jesus healed all ten of the men, but not all of them remembered to thank him.

Jesus Loves the Children

Matthew 19:13–15; Mark 10:13–16

Help the children find their way to Jesus.

Many parents brought their children to Jesus. They wanted Jesus to touch their children and bless them. The disciples thought Jesus was too busy to see the children so they tried to stop the parents from coming. But Jesus said, "Let the children come to me."

THE RICH YOUNG RULER

Matthew 19:16–29; Mark 10:17–30

Color this picture.

A rich young man once asked Jesus what he had to do to be saved. Jesus told him to obey all the commandments. The man said, "I've already done that." Then Jesus said, "Sell everything you have and give your money to the poor." The young man didn't want to do that, so he sadly left Jesus.

A Man In A Tree

Luke 19:1–10

Connect the dots to finish the picture.

Jesus came to Jericho and a man named Zacchaeus wanted to see him. But Zacchaeus was so short that he couldn't see over the crowd of people who had gathered. Zacchaeus climbed a tree so he could see Jesus. He was surprised when Jesus told him to come down. Jesus wanted to come to Zacchaeus' house for lunch.

A GREAT VIEW

Luke 19:1–10

Figure out the secret code to see how Zacchaeus solved his problem.

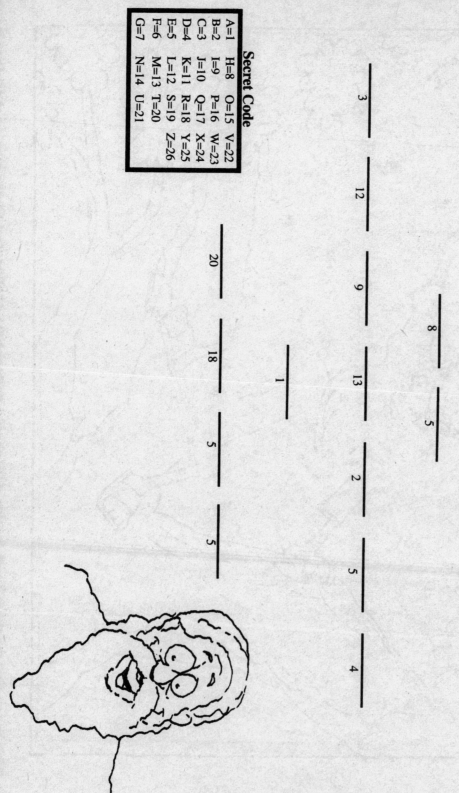

____ ____ ____   ____ ____
3   12   9   8   5

____ ____ ____ ____   ____ ____
13   2   5   4   1

____ ____ ____
20   18   5

Secret Code

A=1	H=8	O=15	V=22
B=2	I=9	P=16	W=23
C=3	J=10	Q=17	X=24
D=4	K=11	R=18	Y=25
E=5	L=12	S=19	Z=26
F=6	M=13	T=20	
G=7	N=14	U=21	

Zacchaeus really wanted to see Jesus, but since he was so short, he couldn't see over the crowd. How did Zacchaeus solve the problem?

Hiding Your Light

Matthew 5:14–15; Luke 8:16

Use the code below to color the picture.

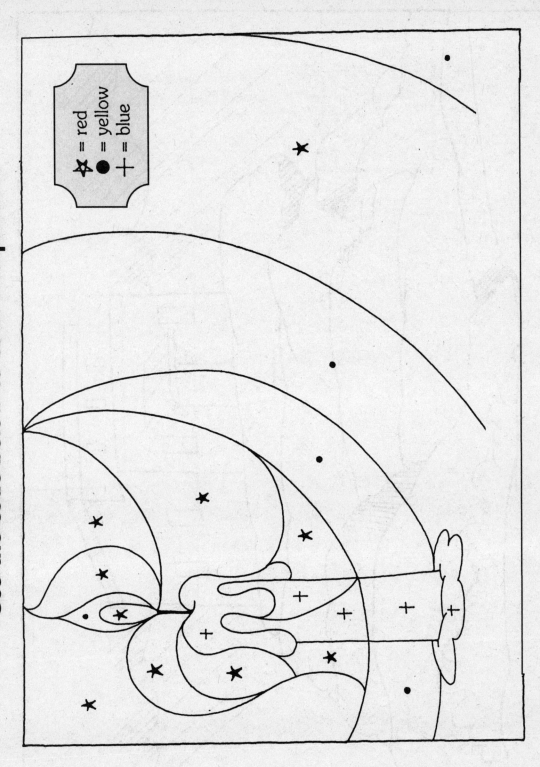

☆ = red
● = yellow
✝ = blue

Jesus taught people by telling them stories. He wanted people who believed in him to know that they are the light of the world. They shouldn't hide their lights under a bowl or a basket. Everyone who loves God should let their light shine so the whole world knows.

THE HOUSE BUILT ON A ROCK

Matthew 7:24-27; Luke 6:47-49

Color this picture.

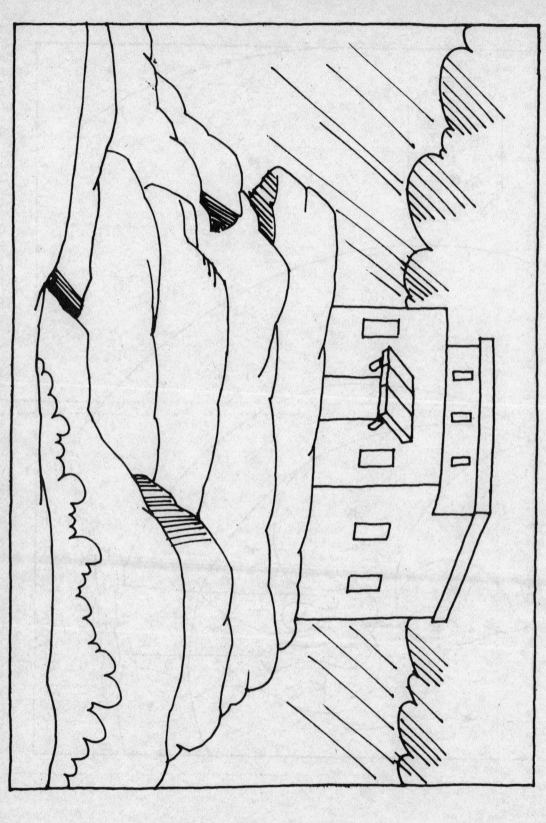

Jesus said that anyone who listened to his teachings and put them into practice was like a wise man who built his house on a rock. A house on a rock would stand firm in a storm, but a house built on sand would fall down in a storm.

GOOD GROWING CONDITIONS

Matthew 13:3–8, 18–23; Luke 8:5–8, 11–15

These two pictures look the same, but there are five differences in the second picture. Circle the differences you find.

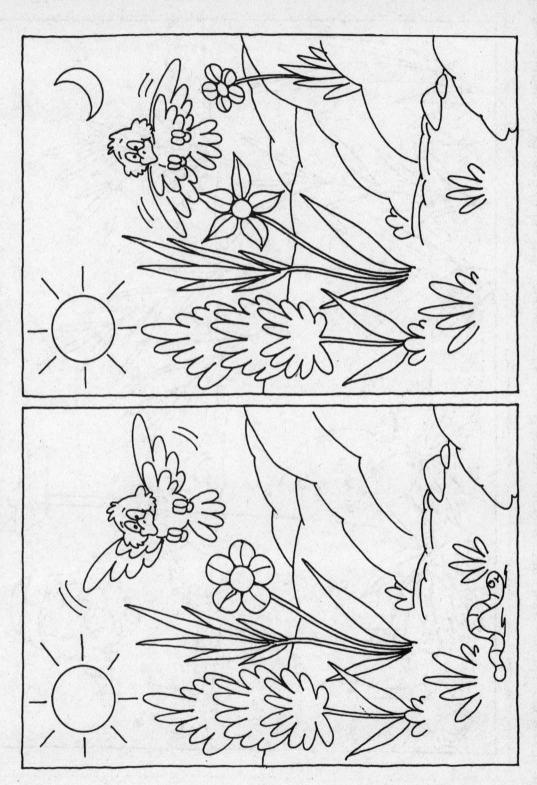

When seeds fall on rocky ground, they can't grow roots. Seeds that try to grow where there are weeds get choked out by the weeds. But seeds planted on good soil grow good plants.

GOOD PLANTS AND WEEDS

Matthew 13:24-30, 36-43

Connect the dots to complete this picture.

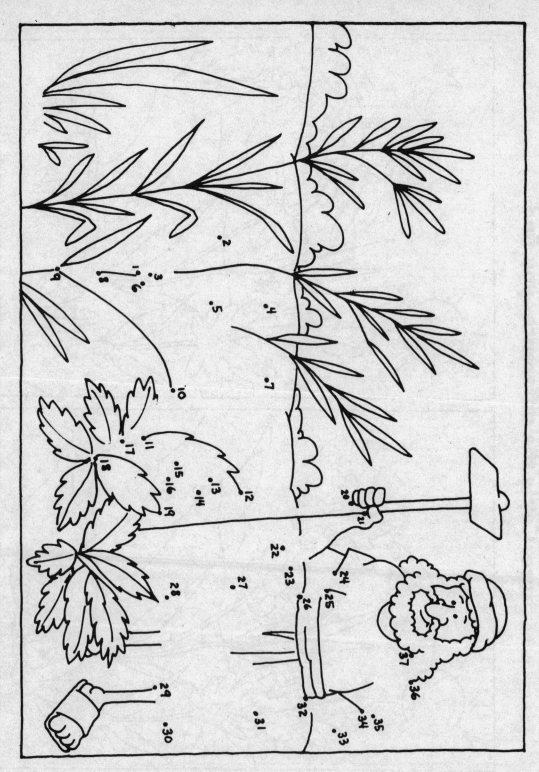

A farmer planted good seed in his field, but while he was sleeping another man came and planted weeds in the same field. The farmer's servants wanted to pull up the weeds, but the farmer said to wait until harvest time. Then the good plants would be separated from the weeds.

THE MUSTARD SEED

Matthew 13:31-32; Mark 4:30-32

Break the secret code to see which small seed can grow into a big garden plant.

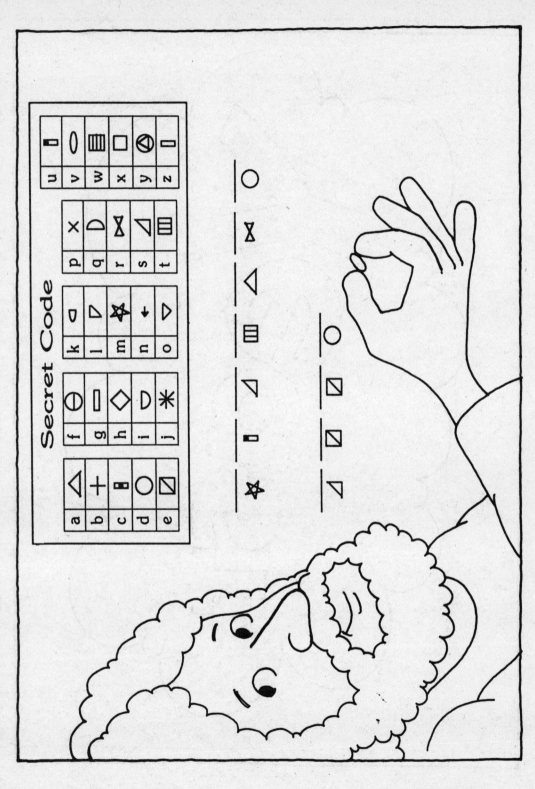

Jesus said that the kingdom of heaven is like a small seed that grows into a big plant. God's kingdom began very small, but it is growing all the time.

GOD'S KINGDOM GROWS

Matthew 13:33

Trace over the dotted lines of this word.

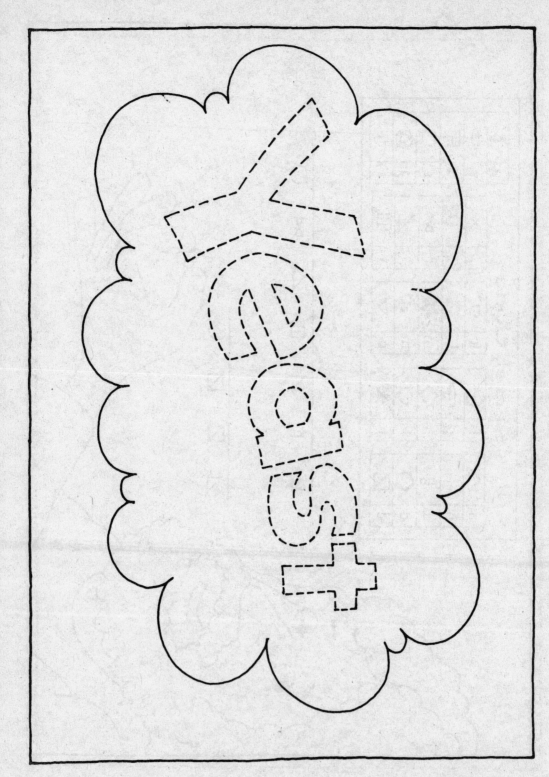

Jesus said that the kingdom of God is like yeast that a woman mixes into her dough. The yeast makes the bread rise and grow bigger. God's kingdom grows bigger every day.

ONE LOST SHEEP

Matthew 18:12–14; Luke 15:4–7

Color this picture.

There was a shepherd who had 100 sheep, but one of the sheep was lost. The shepherd looked and looked until he found the one lost sheep. Every single sheep was important to the shepherd. Jesus cares about everyone, just as the shepherd cared about every single sheep.

VINEYARD WORKERS

Matthew 20:1-16

Use the clues in the box to complete the crossword.

1. Who hired the workers?
2. How much were the workers paid?
3. Where were the workers to do their work?
4. The unhappy workers had been hired ____.
5. The happy workers were hired ____.

1 = landowner
2 = denarius
3 = vineyard
4 = first
5 = last

A landowner hired some men to work in his vineyard. Each worker was paid a denarius for the day's work. The ones who were hired in the morning did not think it was fair that the men who only worked a half day received the same pay for a half day's work.

Two Sons

Matthew 21:28-32

Trace over the dotted lines to finish this picture.

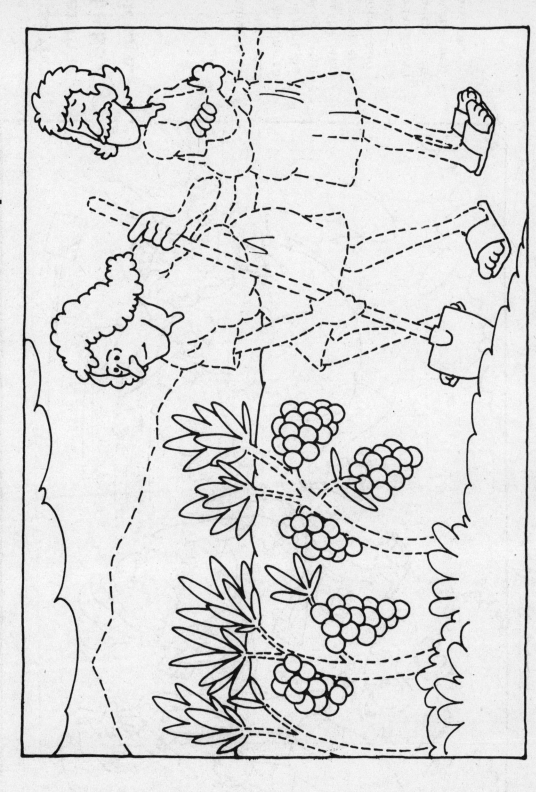

There was a man who had two sons. He asked the first son to do some work in the family vineyard, but the son would not. However the boy later changed his mind and did the work. The father asked his second son to work in the vineyard. He said he would go, but he later decided not to go. God wants us to actually do what he asks, not just say that we will.

Find the shapes that are in the box in the picture.

DISHONEST TENANTS

Matthew 21:33–44

A man rented his vineyard to some men. When it was time to collect their rent, he sent servants to get the money. But the men beat up one servant, killed another, and threw stones at the third. So the landowner sent his son to get the money, but the men killed his son.

A Wedding Banquet

Matthew 22:2-14

Color this picture.

The kingdom of heaven is like a king who prepared a beautiful wedding banquet for his son. Many people were invited, but they all refused to come. So, common people on the street were invited. But, when a man was noticed at the banquet who was not dressed in proper clothing, he was thrown out.

THE FIG TREE

Matthew 24:32-35

These two pictures look the same, but there are six differences between the two. Circle the six differences.

When you see a fig tree with new branches and flowers blooming, you know that summer is very near. It is the same with God's kingdom. When the things Jesus said would happen begin to happen, you know that God's kingdom is near.

The Faithful Servant

Matthew 24:45-51; Luke 12:42-48

Color this picture.

If a landowner puts a servant in charge of his home while he is gone, he expects the servant to take good care of the property and treat other servants fairly. The servant must be faithful, because he doesn't know when the master will return home.

TEN LADIES

Matthew 25:1-13

Color this picture.

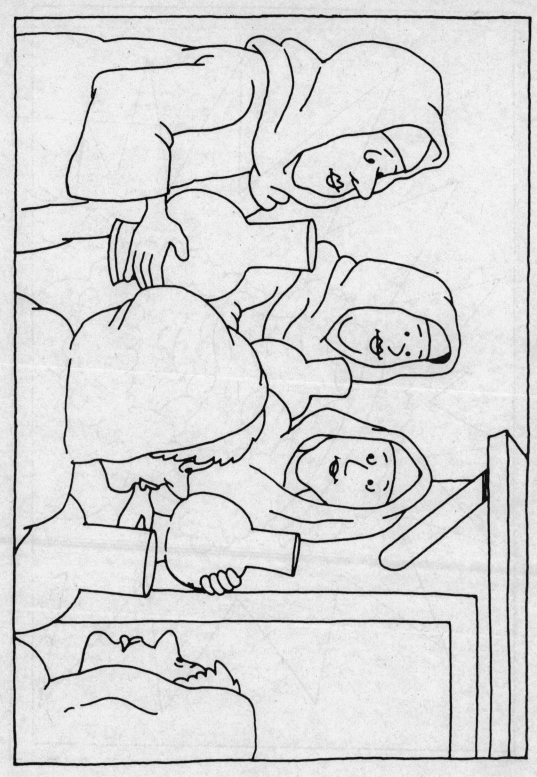

Ten ladies were waiting for their bridegroom to come. Five of them brought along lamps that were full of oil. The other five brought lamps, but didn't bring extra oil. Just before the bridegroom got there, the second five had to leave and buy more oil. They missed seeing the bridegroom because they weren't prepared.

THE PARABLE OF THE TALENTS

Matthew 25:14–30

Unscramble the two mixed up words in this verse so it will make sense.

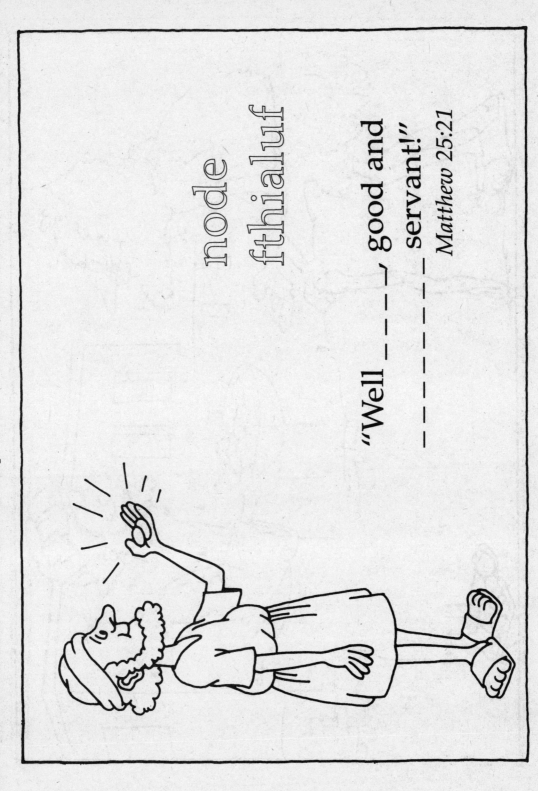

node

fthialuf

"Well _ _ _ _, good and

_ _ _ _ _ _ _ servant!"

Matthew 25:21

A man was leaving on a trip. He gave each of his servants some money to take care of while he was gone. One servant received five talents, the next received two talents, and to the last one he gave one talent. When the man returned he was very happy with the servant who had invested the five talents and doubled it.

SHEEP AND GOATS

Matthew 25:31-46

Connect the dots to complete this picture.

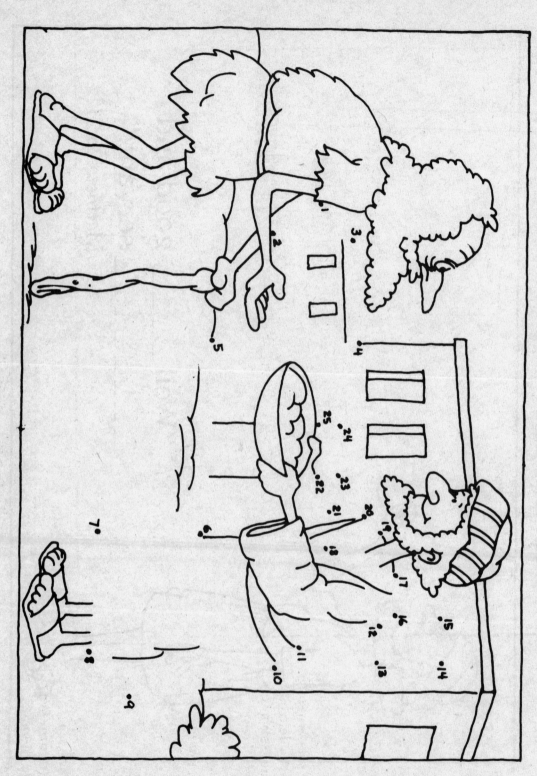

When Jesus comes, he will separate the sheep from the goats. That means he will recognize the people who took care of the poor and needy. When they helped the poor and needy, it was like they were taking care of Jesus.

A WATCHING SERVANT

Mark 13:35-37

Find the items shown in the box in the big picture.

Jesus reminded people that when the master leaves home, his servants should keep watching for him to return. This is an example of how we should always be watching for Jesus to come back because no one knows the day or the hour when he will return. We should always be ready.

FORGIVING DEBTS

Luke 7:41-43

Use the secret code to figure out what this word is.

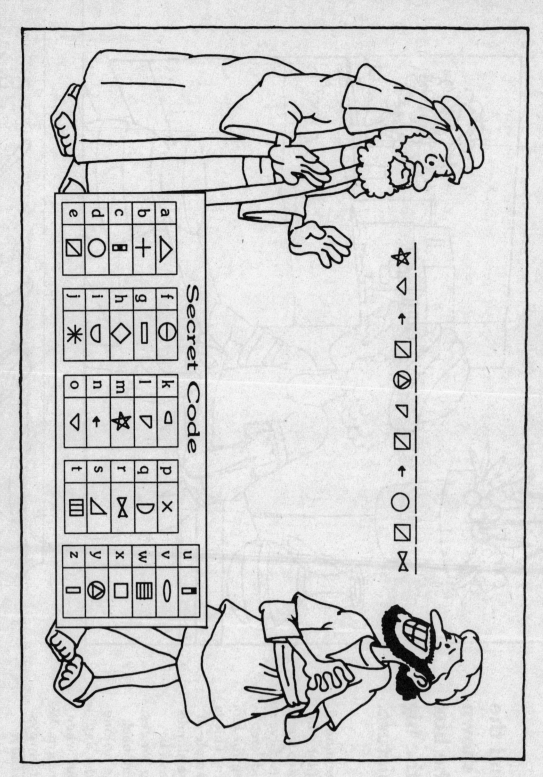

Secret Code

a △	f ⊖	k ◁	p ✕	u ▯
b +	g ▭	l ▽	q ⊐	v ◇
c ▣	h ◇	m ★	r ⋈	w ▤
d ◯	i ⊐	n ↑	s △	x ☐
e ☐	j ✳	o ◁	t ▥	y ⊘
									z ▯

A man loaned some money to two different men. When it was time to pay the money back, neither of the men had enough money. One man owed much more money that the other man did. But the lender forgave both men's debts. Which man do you think appreciated the forgiveness more?

THE GOOD SAMARITAN

Luke 10:30–37

1. Who hurt the traveler?
2. The first person to pass by the hurt man was the ____ .
3. The second person to pass by the hurt man was a ____ .
4. The man who finally helped the hurt man was a ____ .
5. The man paid an ____ to watch over the hurt man.

1 = robbers
2 = priest
3 = Levite
4 = Samaritan
5 = innkeeper

A man was on the way to Jericho when he was attacked by robbers. They left him by the side of the road to die. A priest and a Levite, men who worked for the church, passed by the man. They didn't help him. A Samaritan, who was usually an enemy of this man's people, stopped and helped the man. The Samaritan took him to an inn and gave the innkeeper money to take care of the man.

HELPING A FRIEND IN NEED

Luke 11:5-8

Color this picture.

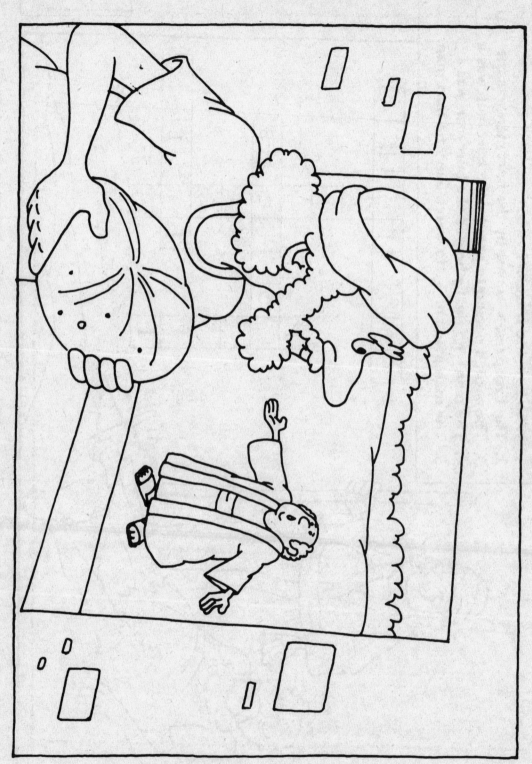

If a friend comes to you late at night and asks for a loaf of bread because he has unexpected company, you wouldn't turn him away. Whatever you ask will be given to you, what you look for, you will find, and when you knock, the door will be opened to you.

THE RICH FOOL

Luke 12:16–21

Trace over these dotted lines to complete the picture.

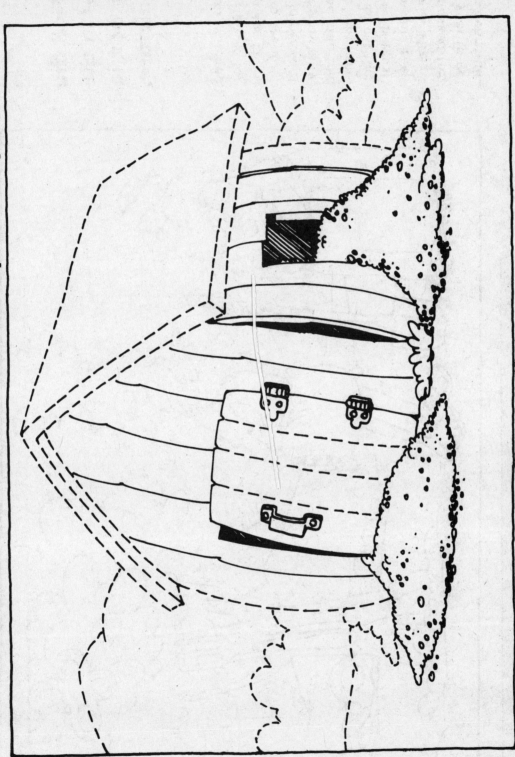

A rich farmer had a very good crop. He had more grain than he had room to store. So, he decided to build bigger barns and keep all the grain for himself. That would make life easy for him in the future. God said that the man was a fool to save the grain for his own use because he would die that very night.

THE UNFRUITFUL FIG TREE

Luke 13:6-9

Find the items in the key box in the picture.

A man had watched a certain fig tree for three years. He wanted to see if it was growing fruit. It never did grow any fruit. So the man told the caretaker of the vineyard to cut the tree down. "It's just using up soil," the man said. The caretaker asked for one more year to get the tree to bear fruit.

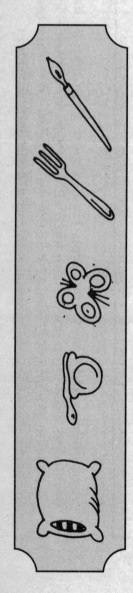

THE LOST COIN

Luke 15:8–10

Help the lady find her lost coin.

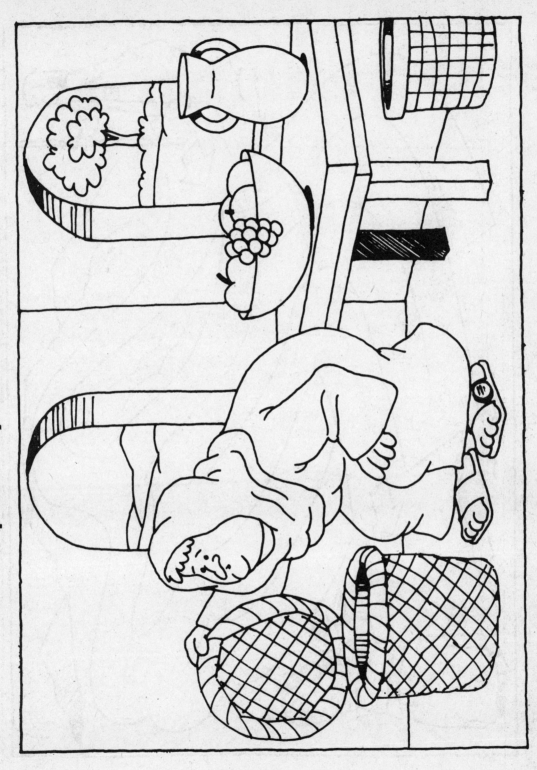

Jesus told a story about a lady who had ten silver coins. She lost one coin. Even though she had nine other coins, she looked everywhere for her lost coin. When she found it, she called her friends to come celebrate with her.

THE PRODIGAL SON

Luke 15:11-32

Help the young boy find his way home to his father.

A man had two sons. The younger son asked for his share of the family inheritance. He left home and wasted all of his money. Before long the young son didn't even have food to eat. He went back home and asked his dad for a servant's job. His father was so glad to see him that he threw a big party.

The Rich Man and the Fool

Luke 16:19–31

Connect the dots to finish the picture.

There was a rich man who lived a life of luxury. Meanwhile, poor sick Lazarus laid under the table hoping to catch a few crumbs from the rich man's food. When they both died, the rich man went to hell. He was able to look up and see Lazarus in heaven, living a good life, so the rich man asked Abraham to send Lazarus to warn his brothers about what was coming.

THE SHREWD MANAGER

Luke 16:1–8

Unscramble the word below for an important message.

y n e o

You cannot
serve God
and
_ _ _ _ _.

A man fired his manager because he wasted his master's money. The manager did not have any other job lined up. So, he let his master's debtors change their bills—that way they would always like him. Jesus said the man made making money more important in his life than God was.

A Big Banquet

Luke 14:16–24

Color this picture.

A rich man was throwing a big banquet. He invited all his rich friends to come, but none of them wanted to. So, he sent his servants out to invite people on the streets to come to his banquet.

Find the shapes in the key box in the picture.

If a servant worked all day in the field, would his master have his dinner cooked and ready for him when he got home? No, the master would wait for the servant to serve him. The servant always does what his master asks.

THE MASTER AND THE SERVANT

Luke 17:7-10

A Persistant Widow

Luke 18:2-8

Trace over the dotted line to complete this picture.

There was once a widow who kept asking a judge to give her justice in a case against her enemy. The judge didn't fear God and he kept ignoring the woman. Finally he said, "I still don't care about God, but you have kept asking, so I will help you."

THE PHARISEE AND THE TAX COLLECTOR

Luke 18:10-14

Connect the dots to finish this picture.

A Pharisee and a tax collector were both in the temple praying. The Pharisee prayed out loud, thanking God that he was so wonderful and not as bad as other men. The tax collector prayed so humbly that he couldn't even raise his head. God was much happier with the humble tax collector than with the proud Pharisee.

THE TRIUMPHAL ENTRY

Mark 11:1–11

Use the clues in the box to complete the crossword.

1. What city did Jesus enter?
2. Who was traveling with Jesus?
3. (down) What did Jesus send two disciples ahead to get?
3. (across) What did people spread on the ground?
4. What did the people shout?

Jerusalem
disciples
colt
cloaks
Hosanna

Jesus traveled around the country doing miracles. Close to the end of his time on earth, he went to Jerusalem. Two disciples had gone ahead to find a colt for Jesus to ride into the city. The people greeted Jesus like a king, shouting "Hosanna!" and spreading their cloaks on the ground.

JESUS CLEANS THE TEMPLE

Mark 11:15-18

Color this picture.

Jesus went to the temple to worship God. But he got upset when he saw men in the temple selling things and cheating the poor people out of their money. Jesus chased the bad men out of the temple saying, "This is supposed to be a place of prayer!"

Jesus Teaches in the Temple

Mark 11:27–13:2

Starting with number 1, connect the dots to finish the picture.

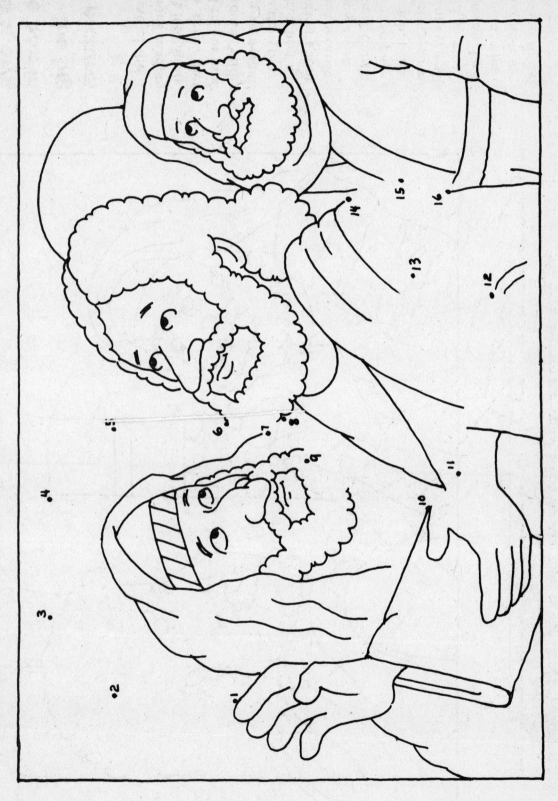

After Jesus cleaned up the temple, he taught the people there about God's kingdom. He often told the people stories (called parables) that showed the point he was trying to make.

WE SHOULD PAY TAXES

Mark 12:13-19

Find the shapes shown in the box in the big picture.

Some of the religious leaders didn't like Jesus. Many times they tried to get him in trouble with the government. One time they asked him a question about taxes because the Jewish people didn't want to pay taxes but the Romans wanted the money. Jesus said to give Caesar, the Roman ruler, what he was supposed to get.

THE WIDOW'S GIFT

Mark 12:41-44

Trace over the broken lines to complete this picture.

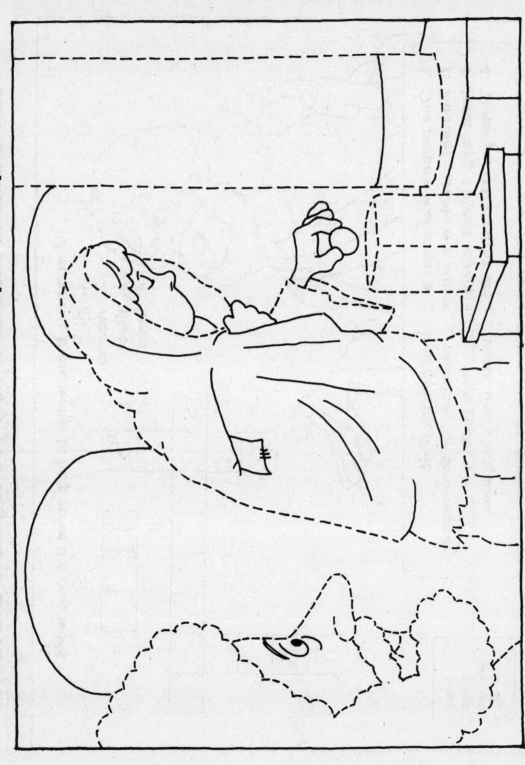

When Jesus was in the temple he saw rich people putting their offerings in the box. Some of them made a big show about the offering they gave. Then Jesus saw a widow lady put two small coins in the box. Jesus told his disciples that the widow gave more than the rich people because she gave all that she had. The rich people gave only their extra money.

MORE PARABLES OF JESUS

Luke 17:11–20:47

Use the clues in the box to help you solve this crossword.

Unscramble these words to help solve the crossword.

1. gfi
2. vsearstn
3. shpee
4. htrtu

1. One parable was about a ___ tree bearing fruit.
2. Another parable was about ___ watching for their master.
3. Jesus taught about separating ___ from goats.
4. These parables taught the ___ about God's kingdom.

fig
sheep
servants
truth

During the last week of Jesus' life on earth, he spent time teaching about God's kingdom. He continued to teach by telling stories or parables.

MARY ANOINTS JESUS

Mark 14:1-9

Color this picture.

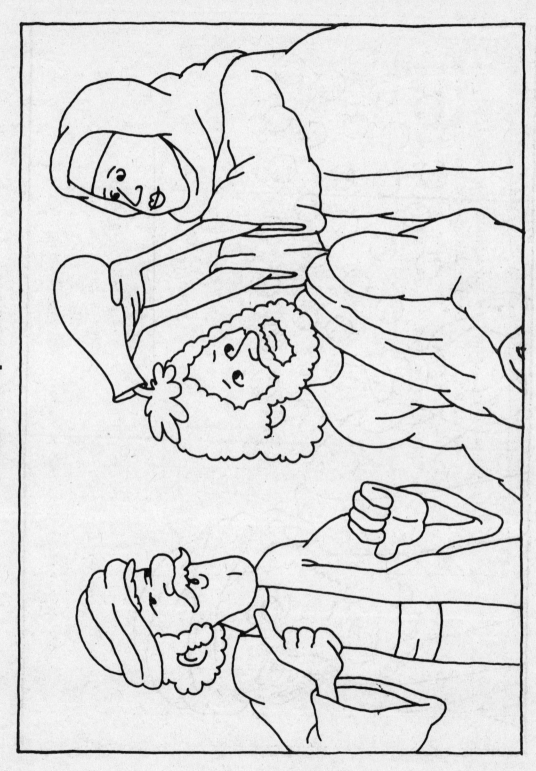

One time Mary came to Jesus with a jar of expensive perfume which she gently poured on his head. Some of Jesus' disciples complained about Mary's action. They thought she should have sold the perfume and given the money to the ministry. But Jesus told them that Mary was anointing him to prepare him for burial.

JUDAS' GREAT DEAL

Matthew 26:14-16

Count how many coins Judas is going to receive. Write your answer on the line.

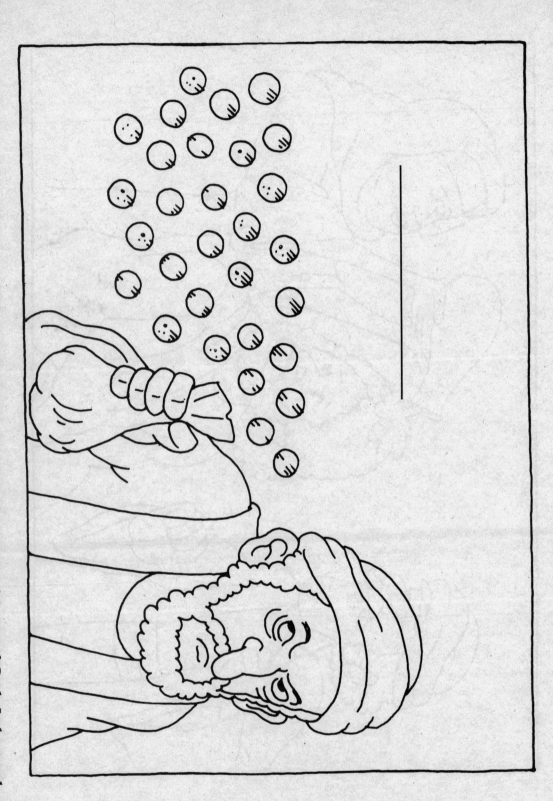

Judas was one of Jesus' disciples, but he didn't really understand that Jesus was the son of God. Judas made a deal with the religious leaders to turn Jesus over to them. He thought that would make Jesus take charge. The religious leaders paid Judas with several silver coins.

PREPARATIONS FOR THE LAST SUPPER

Mark 14:12–17

Find the shapes shown in the box in the picture.

It was almost time to celebrate the Passover meal. Jesus sent two of his disciples into Jerusalem to find a place where they could all eat together. They found a room on the second floor of a building where they prepared the Passover meal.

These two pictures look the same, but the second picture has six differences from the first picture. Can you find the differences?

THE LAST SUPPER

Matthew 26:19-29

Jesus and his disciples ate the Passover meal together. We now call this meal The Last Supper because it was the last time they ate together before Jesus died. At the meal Jesus told his friends that one of them was going to turn him over to the soldiers. His disciples didn't understand what he meant.

The Garden of Gethsemane

Matthew 26:36-46

Color this picture.

When Jesus predicted that one of this friends would turn him over to the soldiers, Judas ran out of the room. Now Judas knew what he was going to do. Jesus took the rest of the disciples to the Garden of Gethsemane to pray with him.

JUDAS BETRAYS JESUS

Mark 14:43-52; John 18:4-8

Trace over the dotted lines to complete this picture.

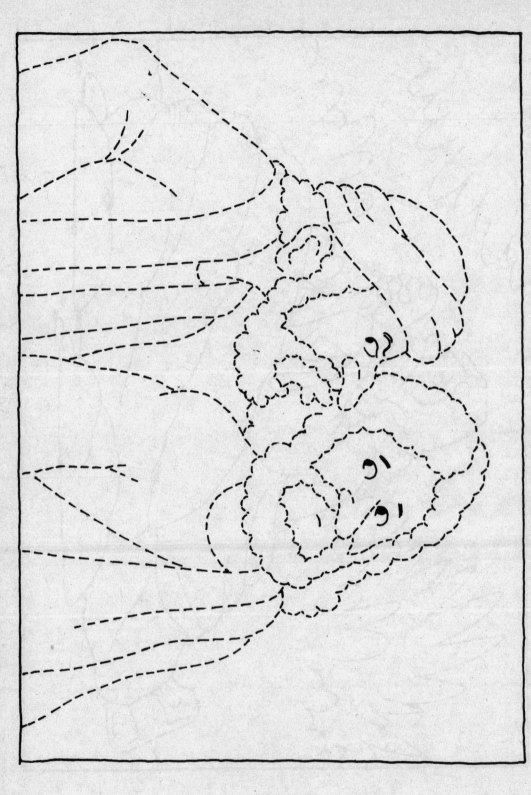

Jesus and his disciples were in the garden praying when Judas arrived with a group of soldiers. Judas came right up to Jesus and kissed him on the cheek. The kiss was a signal to the soldiers that Jesus was the man they should arrest.

Jesus On Trial

Matthew 26:57–68; John 18:13, 19–24

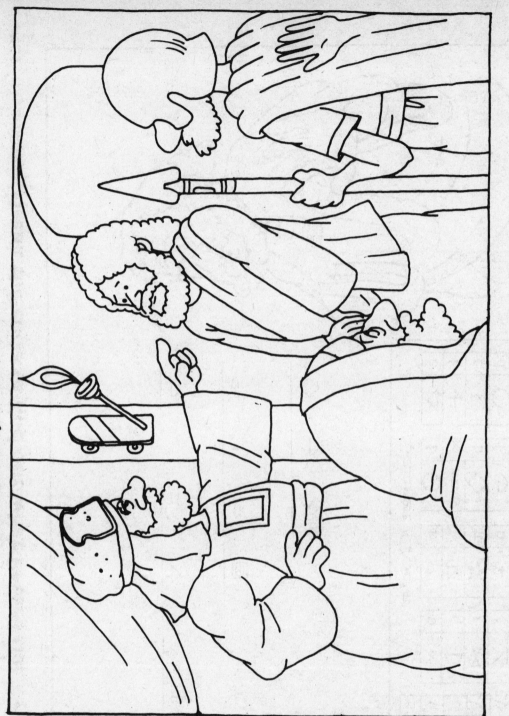

Find the items shown in the key box in the picture.

The soldiers arrested Jesus and took him to Annas, then Caiaphas, then to the council for trial. They all knew that it wasn't right to do this in the middle of the night. But the leaders were afraid that the people would get angry if they knew what was happening.

PETER DENIES JESUS

Matthew 26:58, 69-75; Luke 23:61

Break the code to find out what Peter said.

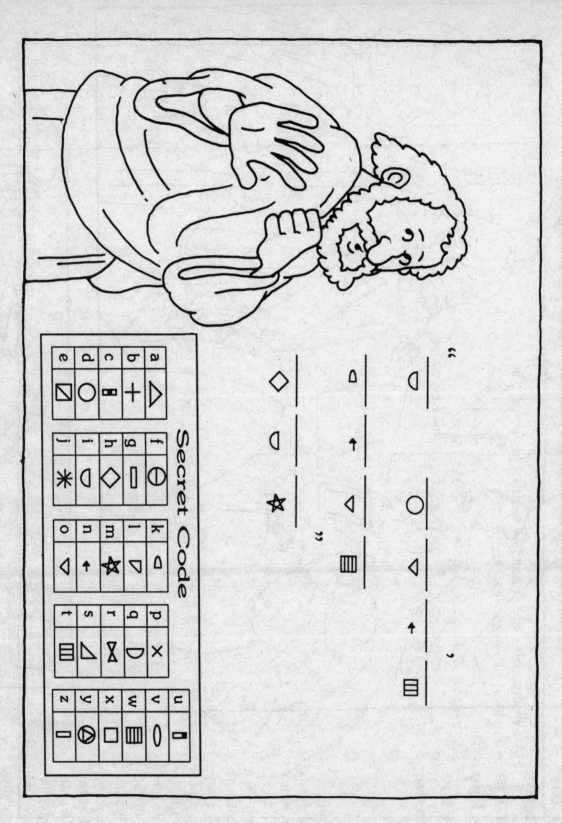

Secret Code

a	◁	f	⊕	k	◁	p	✕	u	⬚
b	✚	g	▽	l	▷	q	⊃	v	▦
c	▣	h	◇	m	☆	r	⋈	w	▤
d	○	i	▭	n	↑	s	△	x	□
e	▢	j	✳	o	◁	t	▥	y	⬡
								z	∕

Three different times during Jesus' trial, people told Peter that they knew he was Jesus' friend. Each time someone said that Peter insisted that he didn't even know Jesus. Jesus had predicted that Peter would do this.

JUDAS' DEATH

Matthew 27:3–10

Use the clues in the box to complete the crossword.

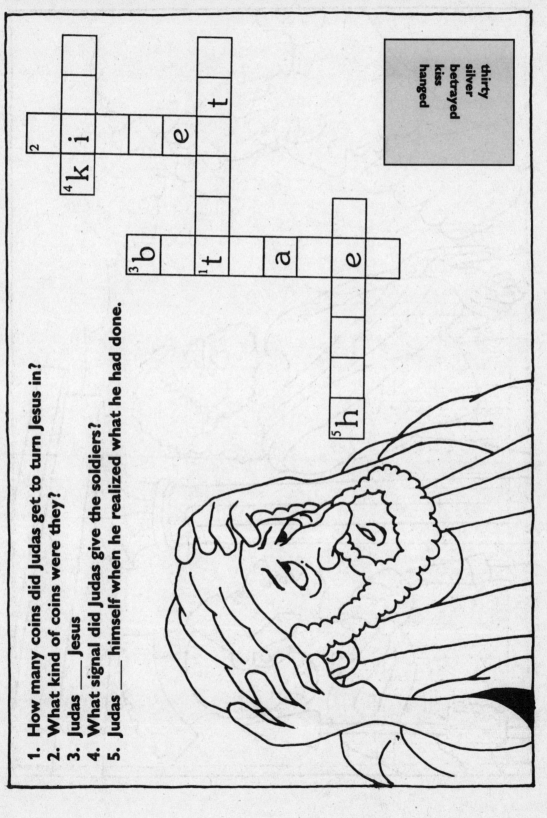

1. How many coins did Judas get to turn Jesus in?
2. What kind of coins were they?
3. Judas ____ Jesus
4. What signal did Judas give the soldiers?
5. Judas ____ himself when he realized what he had done.

thirty
silver
betrayed
kiss
hanged

The council decided that Jesus should die. When Judas realized what he had done he was very upset and filled with guilt. He went out away from everyone and hanged himself.

Jesus Is Sent to Pilate

Color this picture.

The council took Jesus to Pilate, the Roman governor. Pilate listened to the case against Jesus and found no reason to sentence him to death. He even offered to free him. But the crowd of people shouted, "Crucify him!"

Jesus Is Taken to Herod

Luke 23:6-12

Connect the dots to complete the picture.

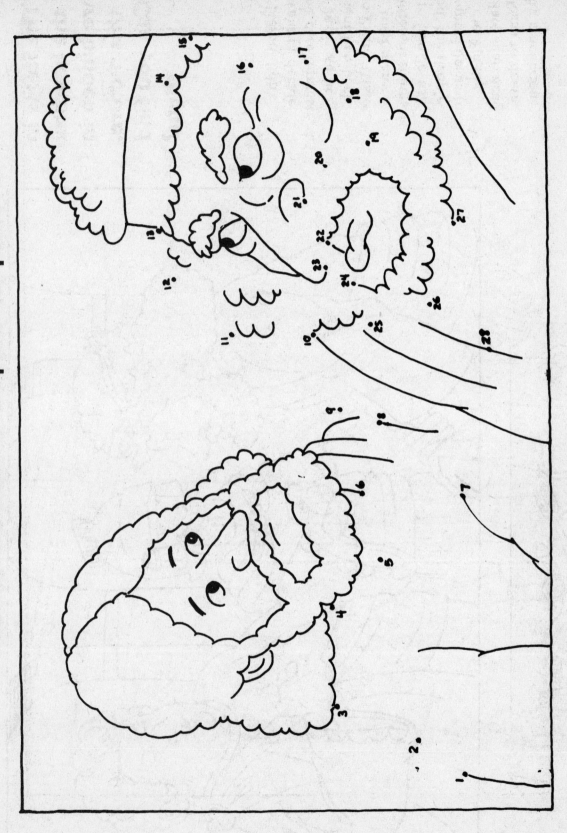

Pilate discovered that Jesus was from Galilee. Pilate didn't rule in Galilee, Herod did. So Pilate sent Jesus to Herod. Jesus wouldn't even talk to Herod so Herod and his soldiers made fun of Jesus.

THE SENTENCING

Luke 23:11-25

The items in the key box are hidden in this picture. Can you find them?

Herod didn't want to decide the case against Jesus, so he sent him back to Pilate. Pilate tried many different things to free Jesus, but the people wanted Jesus to die. Finally, Pilate sentenced Jesus to death by crucifixion.

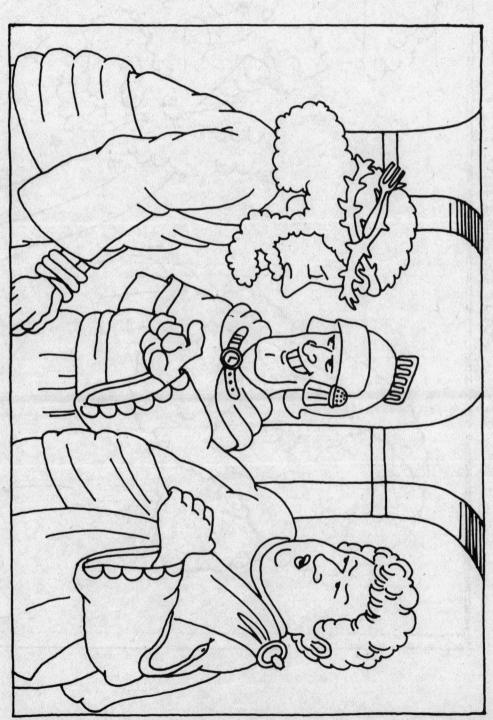

THE CROSS

Luke 23:26-43

Color this picture.

The soldiers made Jesus carry a heavy wooden cross to a place called Golgotha. He was crucified there with a thief on either side of him. Many of his family and followers were there, but they couldn't stop the crucifixion.

THE DAY JESUS DIED

Luke 23:44-49

Color this picture.

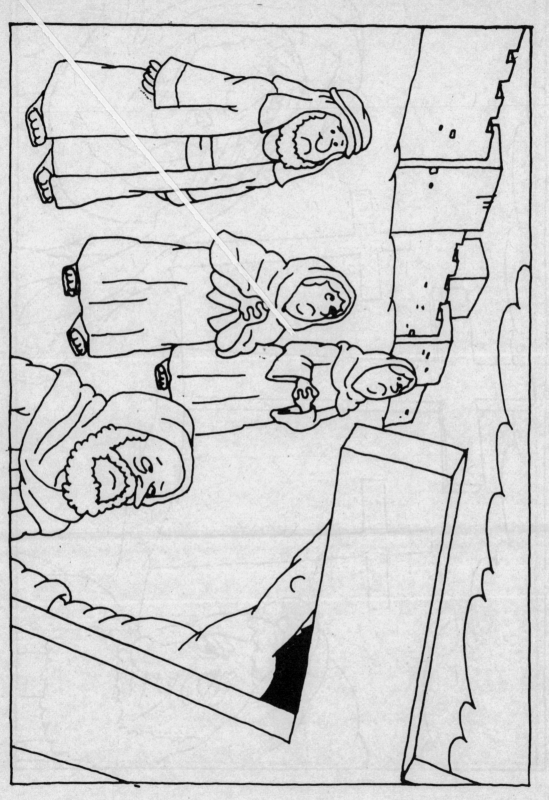

Jesus died when he was nailed to the cross. He was willing to die so that people could be friends with God and live in heaven with him someday.

THE ROMAN SOLDIERS

John 19:23–24

Connect the dots to complete this picture.

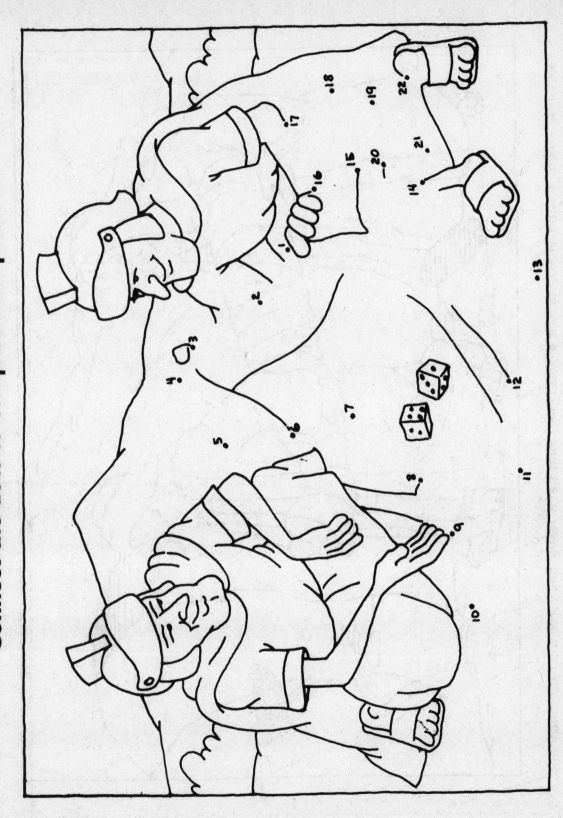

The Roman soldiers stood near the cross and watched Jesus die. They even tossed dice to see which one of them would get to keep his robe. After he died one of them said that Jesus must really be the Son of God.

JESUS IS BURIED

John 19:38-42

Color this picture.

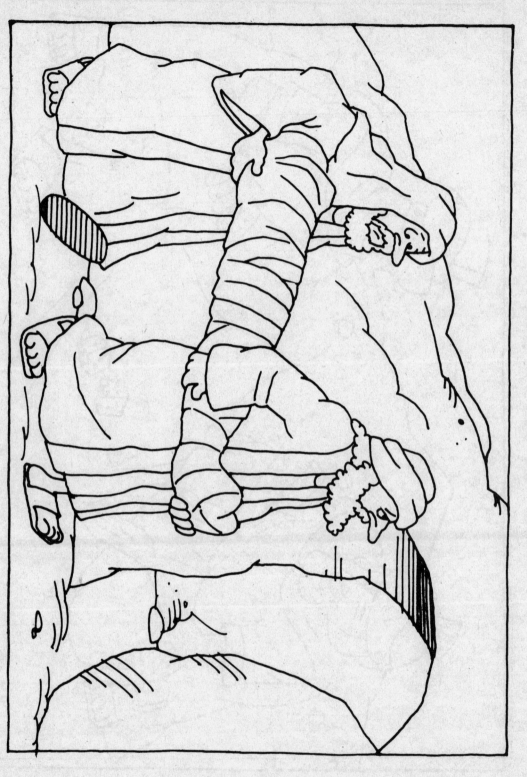

After Jesus died, Joseph of Arimathea asked if he could have Jesus' body. He took the body and buried it in a cave that had never been used before. Then some soldiers rolled a big stone in front of the opening of the cave so that no one could steal his body.

THE WOMEN VISIT JESUS' TOMB

Luke 24:1–8

The women want to go to Jesus' tomb. Can you help them get there?

Sunday morning some women came to the tomb. They wanted to put perfume and spices on his body. The women were worried about how they would move the big stone, but when they got to the tomb the stone was moved and the tomb was empty. An angel told them that Jesus had come back to life!

PETER AND JOHN VISIT THE TOMB

John 20:1-9

Starting with number 1, connect the dots to finish this picture.

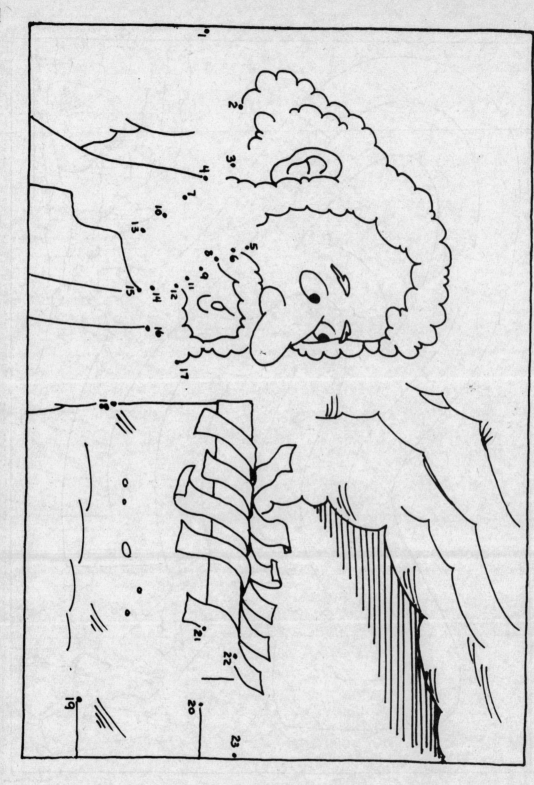

The women ran into town shouting, "Jesus is alive!" The disciples didn't know what to think. Peter and John raced to the tomb to find out for themselves if it was true. Sure enough, the strips of cloth that Jesus' body had been wrapped in were laying on the floor, but Jesus was gone.

MARY SEES JESUS

John 20:10-18

Color this picture.

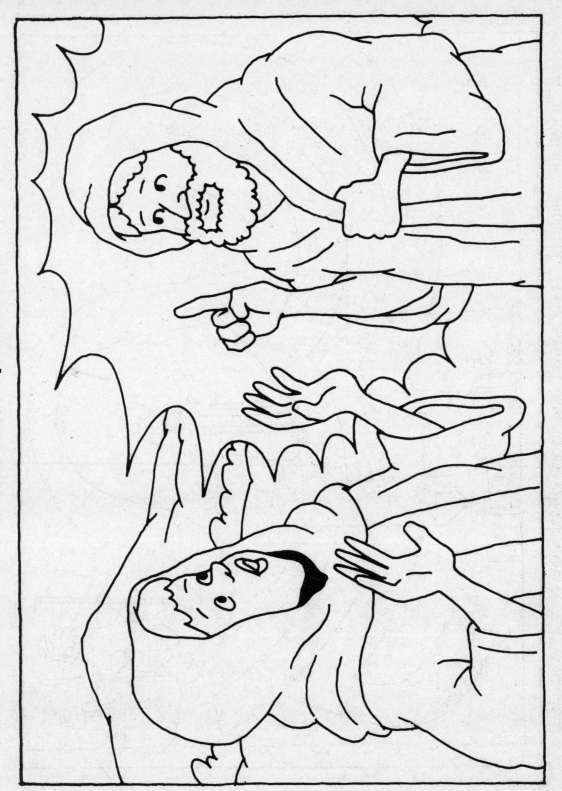

Mary Magdalene was a special friend of Jesus. She was very fortunate to be the first person to see Jesus after he came back to life.

THE ROAD TO EMMAUS

Luke 24:13-35

Help these men on their journey to Emmaus.

Two men were on their way to Emmaus. They were very sad as they talked about the things that had happened in Jerusalem. Suddenly another man came up beside them and asked what they were talking about. They told him and invited him to eat with them. When the man prayed, they realized that he was Jesus!

DOUBTING THOMAS

John 20:24–29

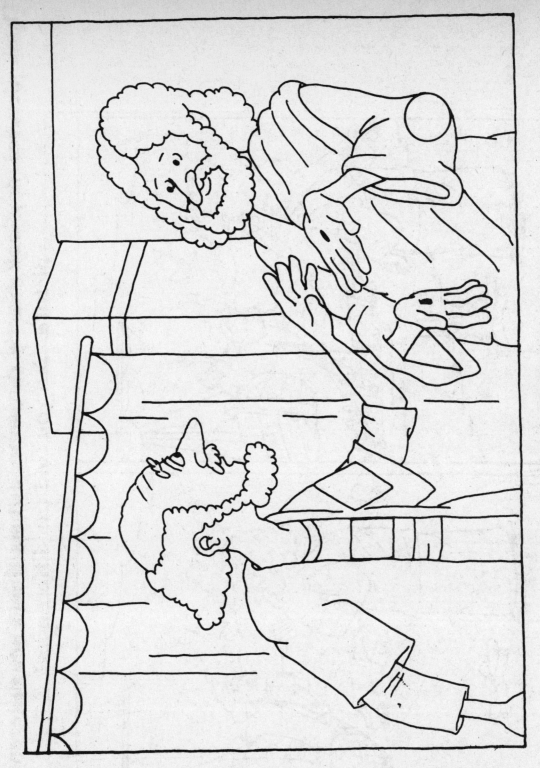

The shapes in the key box are hidden in the picture.

Most of the disciples saw Jesus after he came back to life. But one disciple, Thomas, had not seen Jesus yet. Thomas refused to believe that Jesus was alive until he saw him himself. Jesus came to Thomas and let him touch the wounds in his hands and side.

THE MIRACLE OF THE FISH

John 21:1-14

These pictures may look exactly the same, but six things are different in the second picture. Can you find the differences?

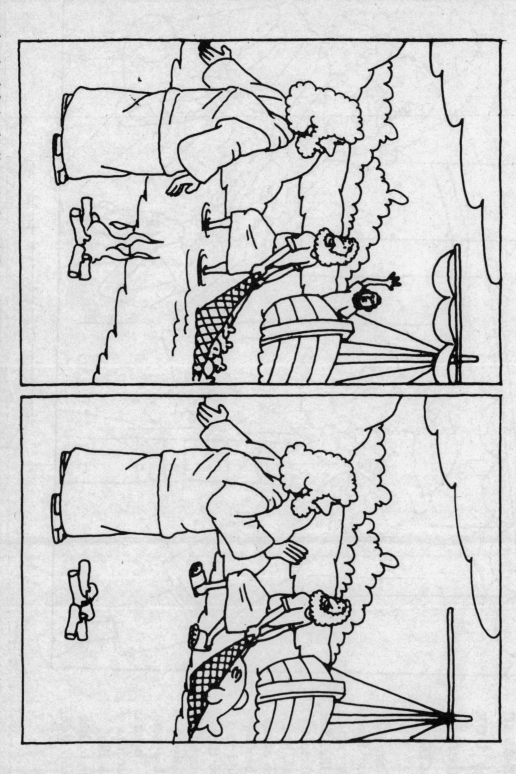

The disciples had fished all night but didn't catch anything. At about dawn they saw a man standing on the shore. "Throw your nets out on that side of the boat," he called, "you'll catch fish there." They did what the man said and they caught more fish than they ever had before. Then they realized that the man on the shore was Jesus.

THE ASCENSION

Luke 24:50-53

Color this picture.

Jesus took his disciples to a place near Bethany. While they watched he was lifted up to heaven. The disciples were filled with joy and happiness and they praised God.

JESUS' LAST WEEK

Luke 19:28–23:56

Use the clues in the box to complete the crossword.

1. (down) Jesus rode into the city of ___ to the cheers of people.
1. (across) A man named ___, one of the disciples, betrayed Jesus.
2. The Roman governor, ___, sentenced Jesus to death.
3. Jesus was ___ on a wooden cross.
4. ___ Magdalene was the first person to see Jesus alive.
5. The women who went to the tomb ran home shouting, "Jesus is ___!"
6. Jesus spent some time with his disciples before he ascended to ___.

Heaven
Alive
Mary
Crucified
Pilate
Judas
Jerusalem

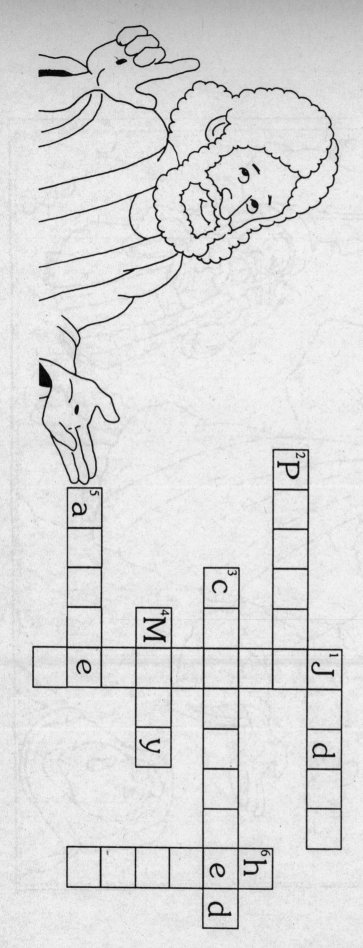

Jesus is in heaven again now. But if we ask him to live in our hearts he can be with us now, too. When Jesus lives in our hearts we can talk to him anytime. Jesus loves us and wants us to love him, too.

PENTECOST

Acts 2:1-41

Connect the dots to complete the picture.

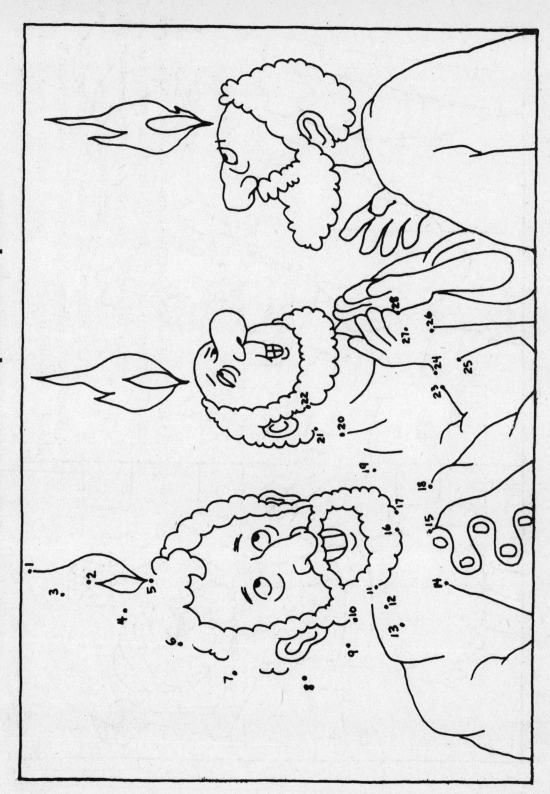

Not long after Jesus went back to heaven, the disciples were all together in a room. Suddenly small flames of fire appeared above the head of each of the believers. It was the Holy Spirit coming to live in the believers, just as Jesus had promised.

PETER AND JOHN

Acts 3

Color this picture.

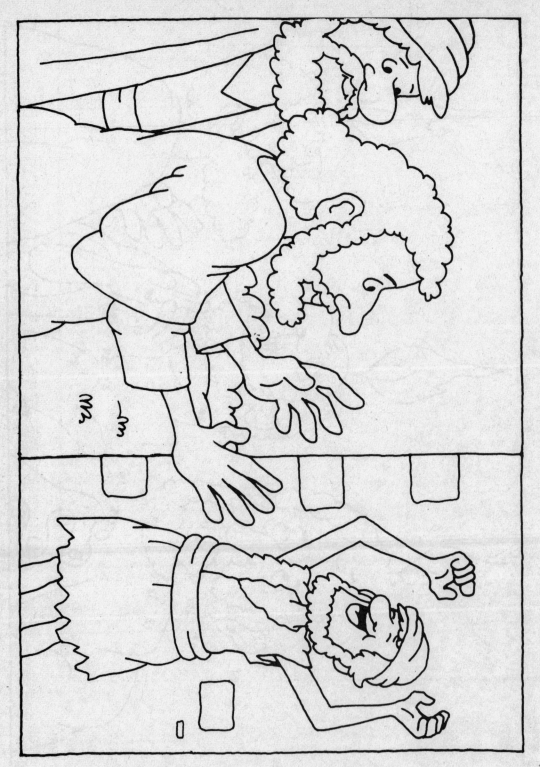

Two of Jesus' followers, Peter and John were going to the temple to pray. A crippled man stopped them and asked them for money. Peter said, "I don't have any money to give you, but in the name of Jesus, stand up and walk!" The man got up and he was healed!

MORE AND MORE BELIEVERS

Acts 4:32—5:16

Find the shapes in the box somewhere in the picture.

The believers stayed close together and helped each other in any way they could. They shared food, clothing and even their homes. They also told other people about Jesus and more and more people believed in Jesus every day.

PERSECUTION OF THE APOSTLES

Acts 5:17-42

These two pictures may look the same, but there are differences between them. Find and circle the differences in the second picture.

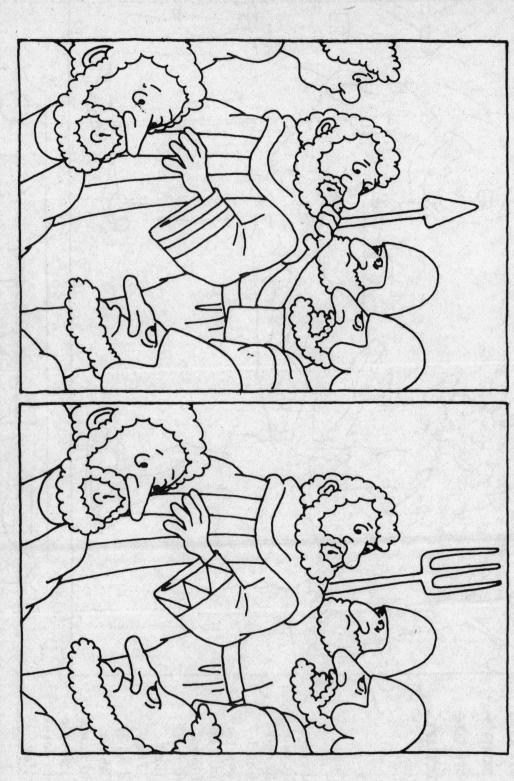

The high priest and some of the other religious leaders were worried about the growing church and the popularity of the apostles. They threatened to hurt the apostles if they didn't stop preaching. But an angel told the apostles to keep on preaching.

The First Deacons

Acts 6:1-7

Use the clues in the box below to solve this crossword.

1. The tension came over who would take care of the ____.
2. Some felt they were not getting enough ____.
3. How many deacons were chosen?
4. The apostles wanted to be free to ____ and preach.
5. One of the deacons was called ____.

widows
food
seven
teach
Stephen

The people in the church started arguing with each other over who should take care of the widows. Some of the widows weren't getting enough food. The apostles were busy teaching and preaching and didn't have time to deal with the arguments. So seven deacons were chosen to take care of problems such as these. One of the deacons was Stephen.

A MARTYR'S DEATH

Acts 6:8—7:60

Connect the dots and you will learn the name of the first man to die as a martyr.

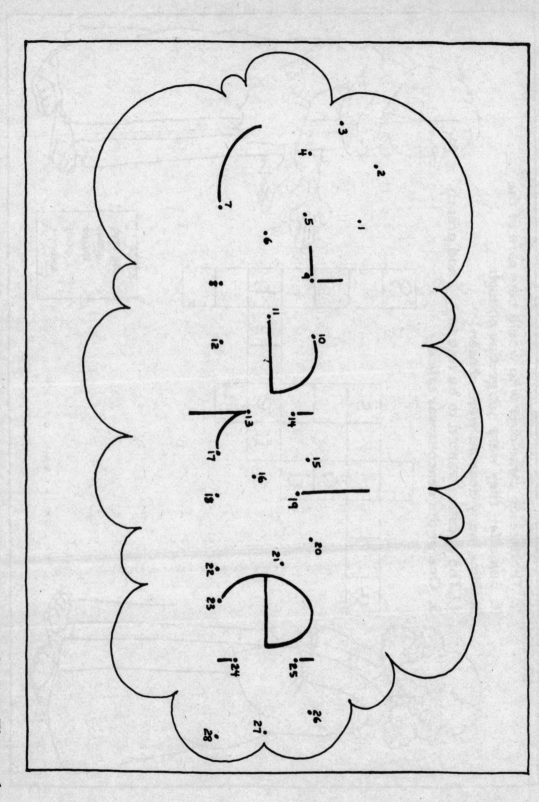

This man did wonderful miracles and told many people about Jesus and how to live for him. This made some people angry and they tried to get him to stop preaching. Even though he was arrested, he kept teaching about Jesus. The people got more angry and threw stones at this man until he died.

Early Church Leaders

Book of Acts

Look in the puzzle for the names of the leaders of the early church which are listed in the box. Circle the names when you find them.

```
J  H  S  T  E  P  H  E  N  I  O  K  J  M  N  B  V
V  D  R  E  F  T  Y  U  J  N  B  G  F  D  C  X  S
W  E  R  T  G  B  N  M  K  L  O  I  J  H  U  Y  G
T  P  F  G  H  Y  U  J  N  B  V  C  X  Z  A  9  Q
W  H  W  9  E  E  D  M  L  K  J  I  U  Y  T  F  F
G  I  E  W  S  D  F  R  E  W  S  X  H  A  9  W  E
D  L  G  P  E  T  E  R  K  J  H  T  G  B  R  E  L
D  I  X  Z  C  V  N  O  P  O  U  Y  H  A  K  L
O  P  U  I  O  L  M  B  M  F  G  T  R  R  W  S
D  F  G  Y  T  H  U  Y  I  H  S  U  T  G  N  R  E
D  S  X  C  V  F  G  T  R  T  I  U  I  O  A  K  M
P  A  U  L  N  B  G  F  L  C  D  E  B  R  E  J
W  N  B  V  F  G  H  Y  T  R  A  D  F  R  A  I  J
H  C  O  R  N  E  L  I  U  S  W  9  A  S  Z  X
C  D  E  W  S  F  H  L  J  O  I  U  Y  T  G
B  V  C  X  D  E  R  T  G  F  D  S  X  C  V  B  U
```

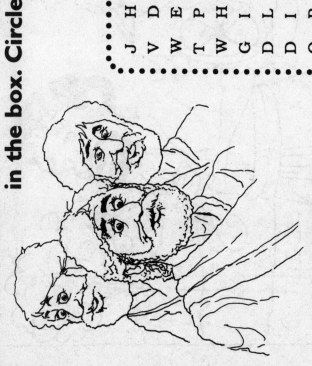

Word Box

PETER

SILAS

PAUL

TIMOTHY

BARNABAS

STEPHEN

PHILIP

CORNELIUS

Find the things shown in the box in the big picture.

Philip's job was telling people about Jesus. One time an angel told Philip to talk to a man riding in a chariot. The man was reading the Bible but he didn't understand it. Philip explained the Bible to the man and the man believed it. Philip baptized the man in a river near the road.

PHILIP AND THE ETHIOPIAN

Acts 8:26-40

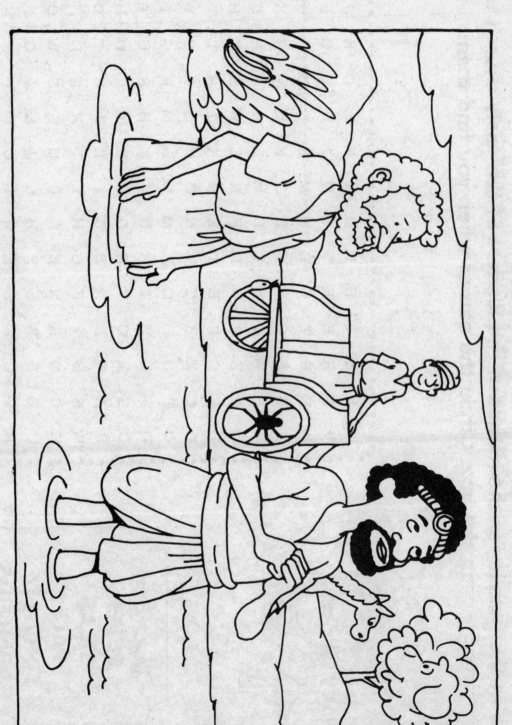

A NEW MAN

Acts 9:1–31

Figure out what Saul's new name is.

SAUL – S + P = _____

Saul hated Christians so much that he hurt them or put them in jail whenever he could. One time Saul was on his way to Damascus, just to put Christians in jail. On the way Jesus spoke to Saul and asked him why he was always hurting him. When Saul became a Christian, Jesus gave him a new name.

An Unusual Trip

Acts 9:1-22

Help Paul complete his journey to Damascus.

Paul was on his way to Damascus to arrest the Christians there when Jesus spoke to him. Paul became a Christian himself after that and spent the rest of his life telling others about Jesus.

One Way Out

Acts 9:23–31

Connect the dots to complete this picture.

Soon after Paul's conversion an angry crowd came after him. The only way he could escape was by having his new Christian friends lower him over the wall of the city in a basket.

DORCAS

Acts 9:36-42

Connect the dots to complete this picture.

Dorcas had many friends and she did nice things for them. She sewed clothes for people and helped them in any way that she could. But when Dorcas got sick and died her friends were very sad. They went to Peter and asked him to help. Peter used the power of the Holy Spirit and raised Dorcas from the dead.

PETER IN PRISON

Acts 12:1-23

These two pictures look exactly the same, but they aren't. Circle the five differences you can find.

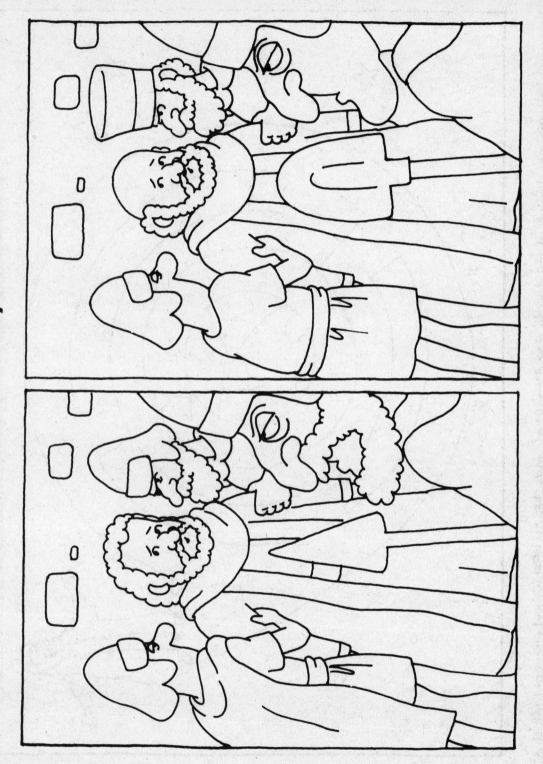

Believers were persecuted for their faith more and more often. Many were even killed because they believed in Jesus. Herod had James killed for his faith and he threw Peter into prison.

PAUL TRAVELS FOR JESUS

Help Paul get started on his first missionary journey.
Acts 13

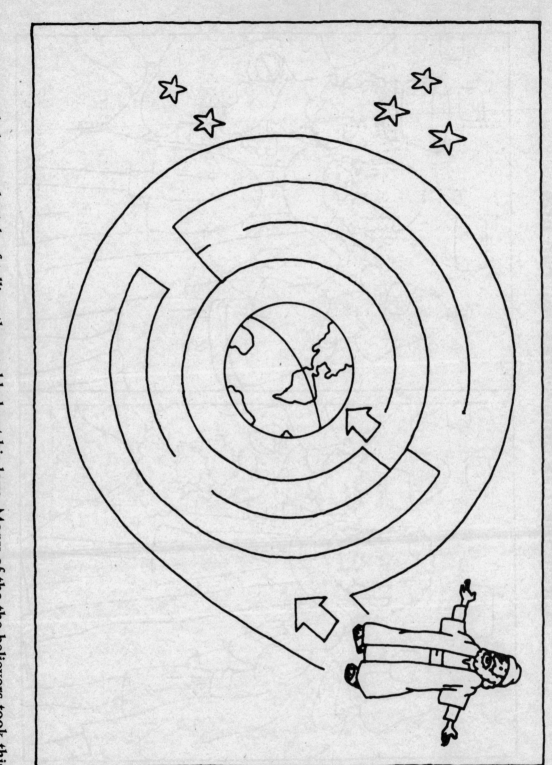

Jesus gave believers the job of telling the world about his love. Many of the the believers took this responsibility very seriously. The church in Antioch sent Paul and Barnabas out as their missionaries. They traveled to other lands to tell people about Jesus.

Mistaken for Gods

Acts 14

Color this picture.

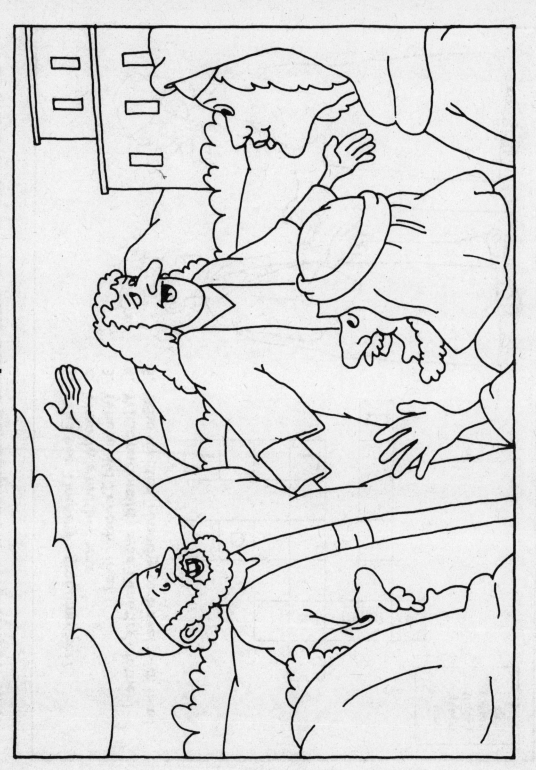

Paul and Barnabas traveled around telling people about Jesus. They even did some miracles. When they healed a crippled man at Lystra, the people thought they were gods. But Paul and Barnabas insisted that they were just normal men who wanted to tell people about the true God.

TIMOTHY

Acts 16:1–4; 2 Timothy 1:5

Use the clues in the box below to help solve the crossword.

1. Who was Timothy's grandmother?
2. Timothy's mother was ____.
3. Where did Timothy live? ____.
4. What nationality was Timothy's father?
5. Who wanted Timothy to travel with him?

Word box:
- Lois
- Eunice
- Lystra
- Greek
- Paul

When Paul was in Lystra on his second missionary trip, he met a young man named Timothy. This young man's father was Greek, but his mother Eunice, and grandmother, Lois had taught him about Jesus. Paul asked Timothy to come and travel with him.

A SPECIAL REQUEST

Acts 16:6–10

Break the secret code to find out where Paul went.

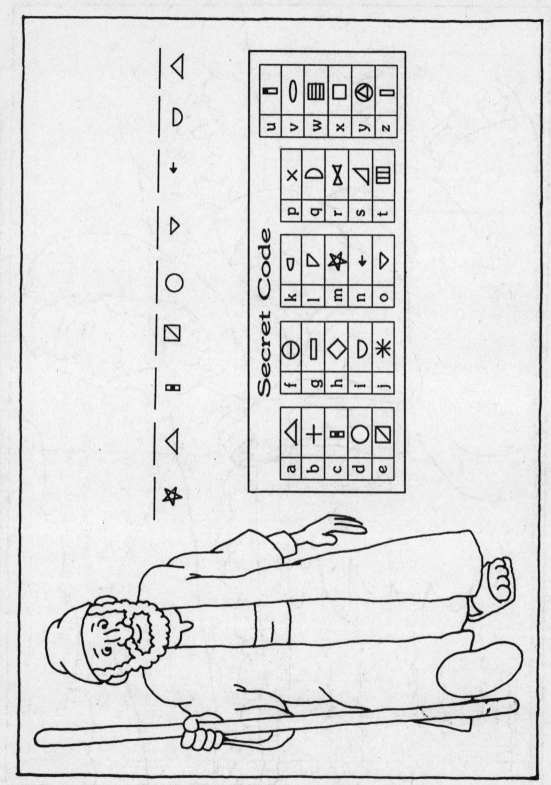

Secret Code

Silas went with Paul on his second missionary journey. When Paul was in Troas, he had a dream about a man asking him to come help his people. Paul and Silas left immediately for that man's country.

LYDIA

Acts 16:11-15

Color this picture.

Paul met a woman named Lydia when he joined a group of women who were praying near a river. The woman listened to Paul's teaching and became a believer. Then Lydia invited Paul and Silas to her home.

THE PRISON EARTHQUAKE

Acts 16:16-40

Connect the dots to complete this picture.

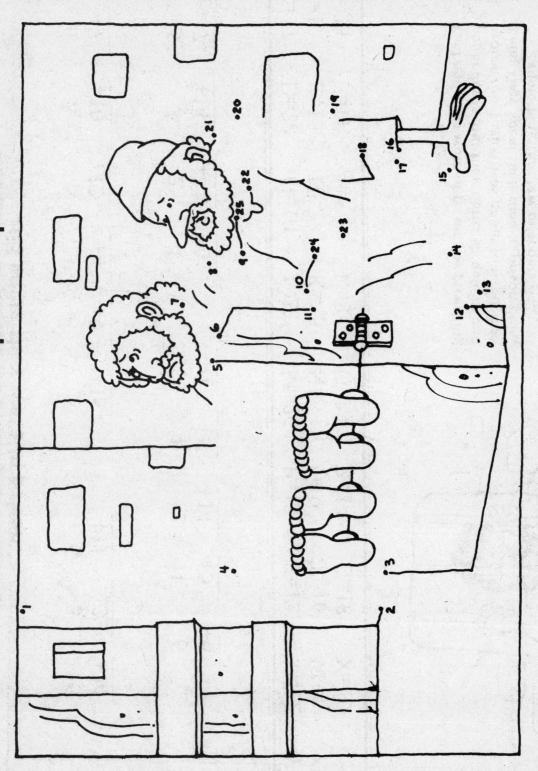

Paul and Silas were in prison because of their faith. Even though it was near midnight, Paul and Silas were singing hymns and the other prisoners were listening. Suddenly an earthquake shook the prison and the doors fell off. All the prisoners could have escaped, but Paul kept everyone in their cells. Later he told the jailer about Jesus, and the jailer and his whole family became Christians.

PAUL AND SILAS IN PRISON

Acts 16:16-40

Add the numbers to solve the code and see what Paul and Silas did while they were in prison.

```
  6      4      5      3      6      5
 +7    +10    +12     +4     +9    +15
```

```
  5      3      2      4      2      1     12     1      6
 +7    +14     +4     +6     +0    +6    +14    +5     +6
```

```
  6      3      6
+11     +3    +14
```

A=17	D=20	G=10	J=22	M=26	P=13	S=12	V=22	Y=7
B=1	E=15	H=2	K=25	N=6	Q=9	T=16	W=4	Z=3
C=23	F=11	I=5	L=8	O=24	R=14	U=18	X=19	

Paul and Silas were in prison for preaching about Jesus. But they didn't sit quietly and worry about what was going to happen to them. They spent their time in prison doing something that few prisoners do.

PAUL IN THESSALONICA

Acts 17:1-9

Trace over the dotted lines to spell the name of Paul's friend.

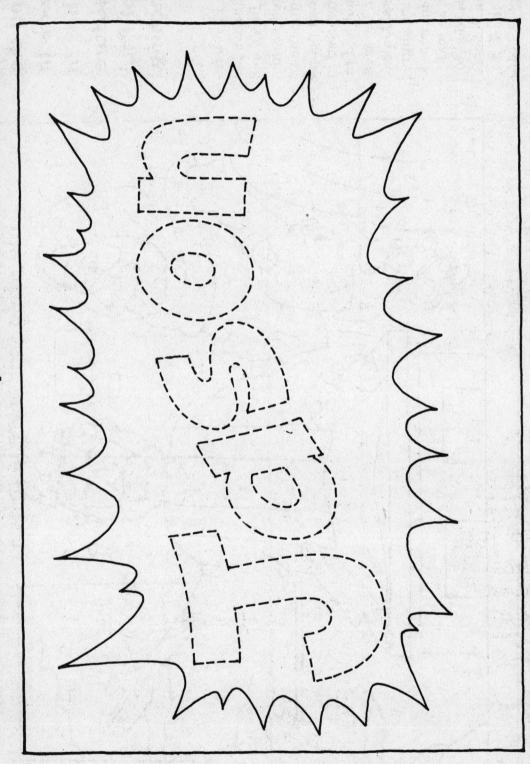

Paul was preaching in Thessalonica. Some men from the synagogue got angry at him and went looking for him. They went to Jason's house where Paul was staying. Paul wasn't there, but they arrested Jason and he had to pay money to get his freedom.

Find the items in the box in the picture of Paul teaching.

PAUL IS ACCEPTED

Acts 17:10-15

When Paul left Thessalonica, he went to Berea and preached in the synagogue there. The Berean people were interested in what Paul had to say. But, the men in Thessalonica who were angry with Paul heard where he was. They hurried to Berea and caused trouble there. So, Paul had to leave Berea, too.

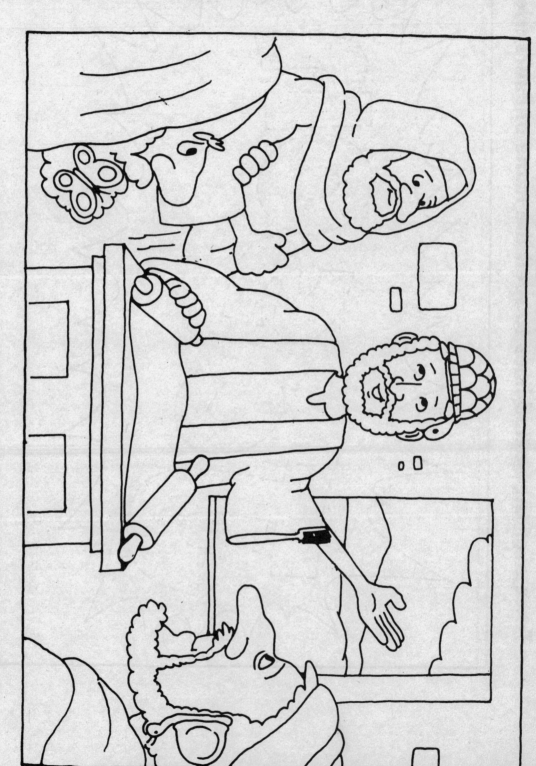

Paul Preaches In Athens

Acts 16:16-34

Unscramble these words to complete this Bible verse.

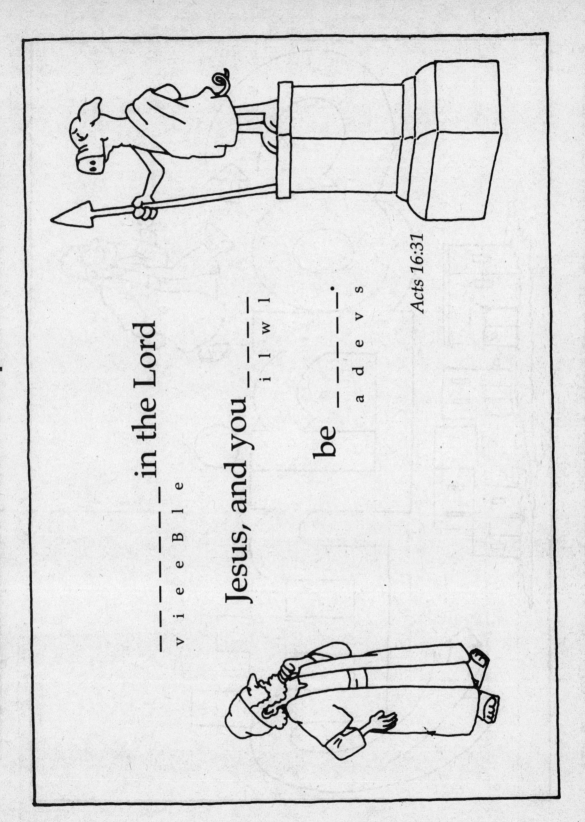

_ _ _ _ _ _ _ in the Lord
v i e e B l e

Jesus, and you _ _ _ _
i l w l

be _ _ _ _ _.
a d e v s

Acts 16:31

Everywhere Paul went he taught about Jesus and told people how they could be close to God.

PAUL IN CORINTH

Acts 18:18-23

Paul wants to preach in Corinth. Can you help him get there?

Paul went to preach in Corinth. He met a husband and wife there named Aquila and Priscilla. They were tentmakers like Paul was. Paul enjoyed talking with them about Jesus.

PAUL AND GALLIO

Acts 18:9–17

Starting with number 1, connect the dots to finish this picture.

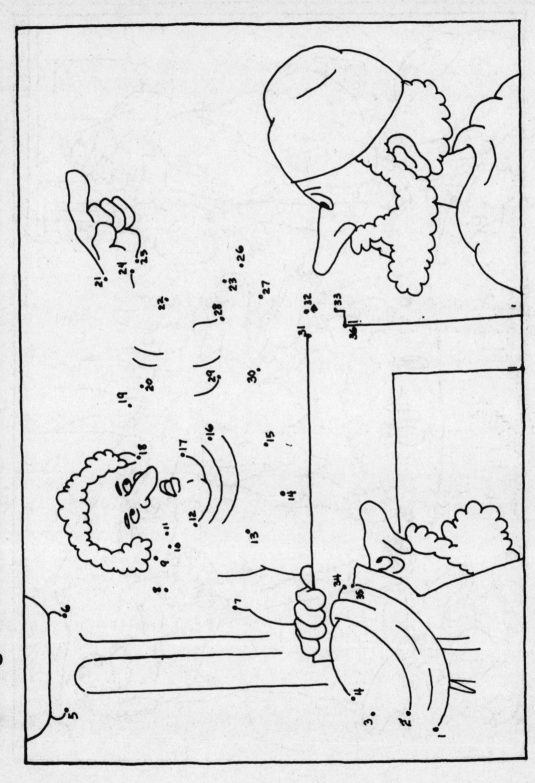

Some people in Corinth thought that Paul was encouraging people to break the law by the ways he taught to worship God. They kidnapped Paul and dragged him to the Roman governor. Gallio, the governor, listened to their complaints, then told them to settle the problem themselves.

THE BOOKS OF EVIL ARE BURNED

Acts 19:13-20

Color this picture.

Paul kept doing miracles and teaching about Jesus. Some Jews had been doing things that did not honor God. When they listened to Paul's teaching and believed in Jesus, they wanted to stop sinning. So they burned the scrolls or books of evil they had been reading.

AN EPHESIAN GOD

Acts 19:23-41

Break the secret code to find out the name of the Ephesian god.

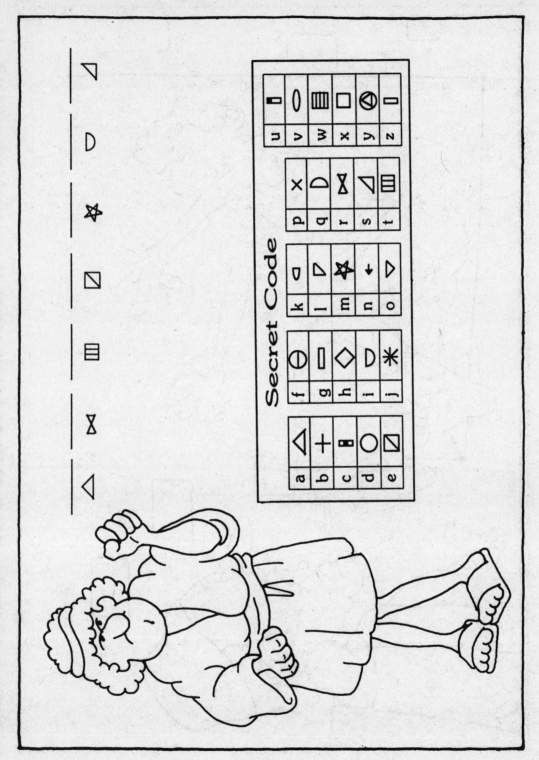

Secret Code

Demetrius earned his living by making silver shrines of an Ephesian goddess. Demetrius got angry with Paul because Paul told people to stop worshiping this goddess. He tried to stir up the crowd against Paul, but it didn't work.

One night a young man named Eutychus was sitting in the window, listening to Paul preach. The young man went to sleep and fell out of the window. The crowd rushed down and discovered that Eutychus was dead. But Paul took his hand and raised him back to life.

Paul Is Arrested

Acts 21:27—23:11

Color this picture.

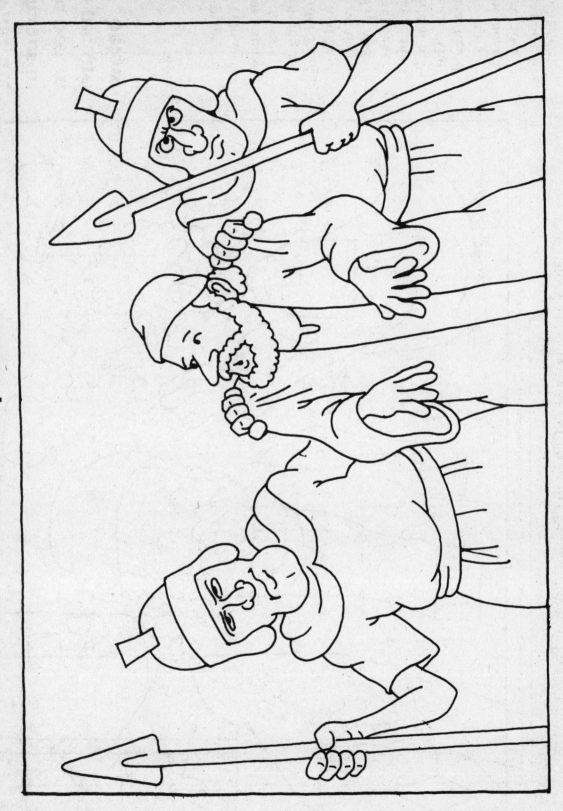

Paul tried to show the people that he remembered he was Jewish in addition to being a Christian. But before long he was arrested anyway.

Find the shapes in the box in the picture below.

Paul Is Warned

Acts 23:12-35

Paul's nephew heard some Jews planning to murder Paul. He told Paul about their plan and Paul sent him to the official in charge. The official heard the story, then moved Paul to a safer place in another city.

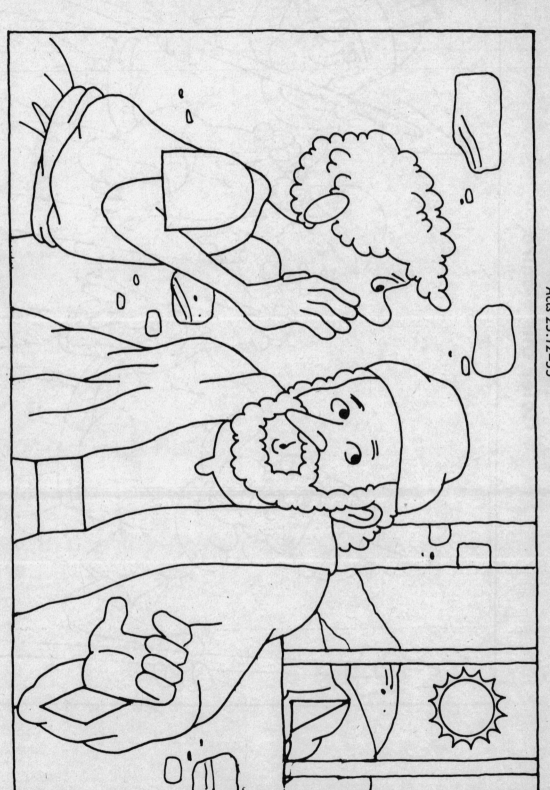

PAUL AND AGRIPPA

Acts 25:13–26:32

Use the color key to color this picture of Paul.

COLOR KEY
1 = red
2 = blue
3 = yellow
4 = green
5 = brown
6 = orange

Paul was a prisoner for about two years. Felix and Festus both heard the case against Paul. Then Paul asked to be judged by Caesar, so Festus sent him to King Agrippa. The king listened to Paul's story of how he became a believer.

PAUL GOES TO ROME

Paul needs to go to Rome to see Caesar. Can you help?

Acts 27:1-12

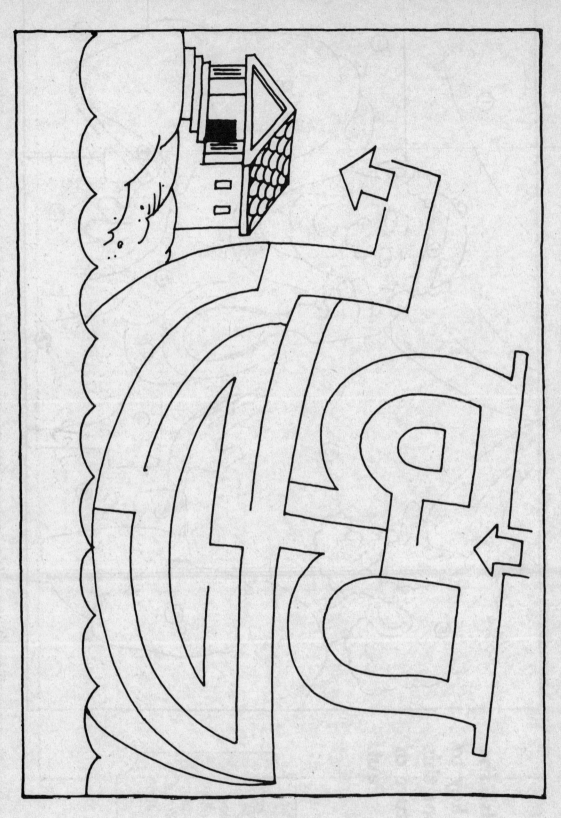

King Agrippa agreed to send Paul to Rome to be judged by Caesar. The trip was made by sailing ship, but it took a long time because there wasn't much wind to move the ship along.

SHIPWRECK!

Acts 27:13–44

Color this picture!

Paul's ship was sailing during a dangerous sailing season. The ship wrecked on a sandbar and the waves broke the ship apart. The soldiers wanted to kill the prisoners to keep them from escaping, but one guard wanted to keep Paul alive, so he protected all the prisoners.

THE LIFE OF PAUL

Book of Acts

Use the clues in the box below to solve the crossword puzzle.

1. Paul used to be called ____.
2. Paul was on the way to ____ when Christ spoke to him.
3. Paul traveled with ____ on his first missionary journey.
4. When some Jews plotted to kill Paul his ____ saved him.

Saul
Damascus
Barnabas
Nephew

At one time Paul spent his time persecuting Christians. Then Paul became a believer and spent the rest of his life preaching about Jesus. His former friends tried to stop him. They even had him arrested. But Paul kept telling everyone he saw about Jesus.

PEOPLE OF THE NEW TESTAMENT

Use the clues and Bible references to figure out the puzzle.

Across

1. He pretended to be Jesus' friend. Matthew 26:46-49
2. He was stoned to death because he loved Jesus. Acts 7
3. Jesus' beloved friend who wrote about the future. Rev. 1:1
4. This man's daughter died, but Jesus brought her back to life.
   Mark 5:22-43
5. The first Gentile who loved Jesus. Acts 10:1
6. She sat and talked with Jesus. Luke 10:38, 39

Down

7. Jesus' friend who died. John 11:14, 15, 43, 44
8. Jesus' follower who doubted he was alive.
   John 20:24, 25
9. She did housework. Luke 10:38-40
10. A small boy gave this to Jesus. John 6:5-13
11. He cut off a soldier's ear to try and protect Jesus.
    John 18:1-11
12. He escaped from his enemies in a basket.
    Acts 9:24, 25

WORD BOX

Stephen	Lazarus
Thomas	John
Jairus	Cornelius
Martha	Mary
Judas	Paul
Lunch	Peter

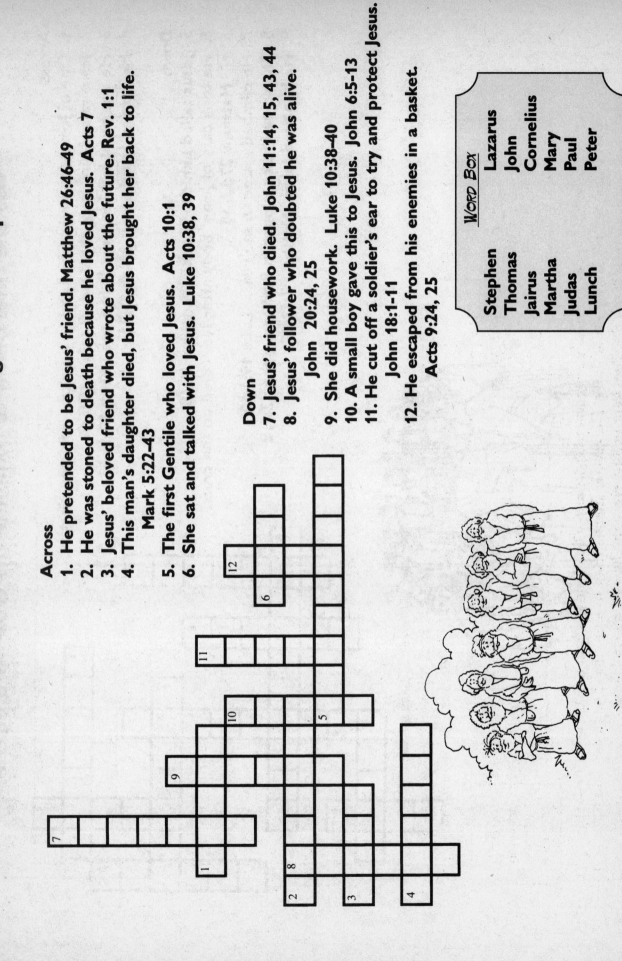

FRIENDS OF JESUS

Use the clues below to complete the crossword puzzle.

Across

1. One of Jesus' followers who used to be a tax collector. Matthew 9:9
2. Jesus raised him from the dead. 2 John 11:38-44
3. He was blind but Jesus made him see. Mark 10:46-52
4. He carried Jesus' cross. Mark 15:21

Down

5. Jesus called him the "Rock." Matthew 16:18
6. He took care of Jesus' body after Jesus died on the cross. Matthew 27:57-60
7. He climbed a tree to see Jesus. Luke 19:1-10
8. She served Jesus supper in Bethany. John 12:1, 2
9. He baptized Jesus. Matthew 3:13-17

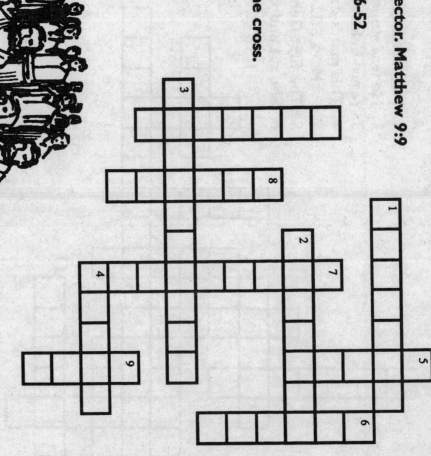

HE IS...

Look for the words from the name box in the puzzle.

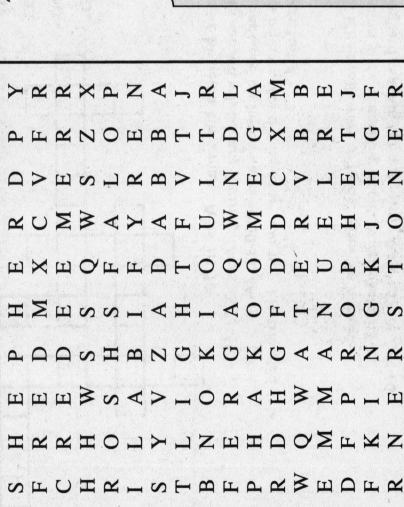

Son	Omega
Light	One
Savior	Lamb
Messiah	Word
Redeemer	Cornerstone
Way	Shepherd
Alpha	Prophet
Truth	Christ
Water	God
Vine	Abba
Lord	Emmanuel
King	Holy
	Jehovah

Jesus is called by many different names in the Bible.

LEADERS OF THE EARLY CHURCH

Use the Bible
references to solve
the puzzle about the
leaders of the early
church. Use the words
in the word box if you
need help.

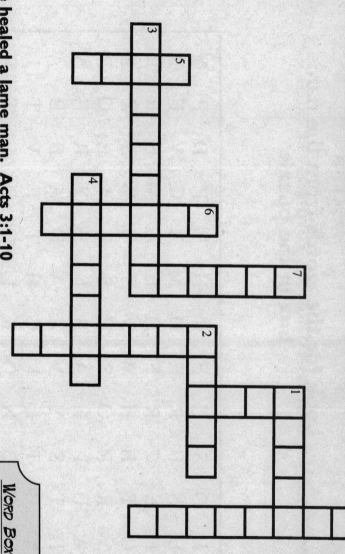

Across

1. After the Holy Spirit came he healed a lame man. Acts 3:1-10
2. He went with Paul on Paul's second missionary journey. Acts 15:36-41
3. A Roman soldier who was baptized by Peter. Acts 10:30-33, 46-48
4. Paul met this man in Lystra on his second missionary journey. He traveled with Paul after that. Acts 16:1-4

Down

1. At one time he hunted and killed followers of Jesus. After he became a believer he traveled far and wide preaching about Jesus. Acts 9:1-22
2. He was stoned for preaching and teaching about Jesus. Acts 6:8-10; 7:54-60
5. He was a disciple of Jesus who was arrested along with Peter for preaching and healing. Acts 4:1-4
6. He met an Ethiopian on the road and baptized him. Acts 8:26-40
7. She had died but Peter raised her from the dead. Acts 9:36-42
8. He traveled with Paul on Paul's first missionary journey. Acts 13:1-3

WORD BOX

Dorcas
Silas
Barnabas
Peter
John
Cornelius
Stephen
Timothy
Philip
Paul

ON THE ROAD FOR JESUS

Book of Acts

Unscramble each word below to discover some of the places Paul went.

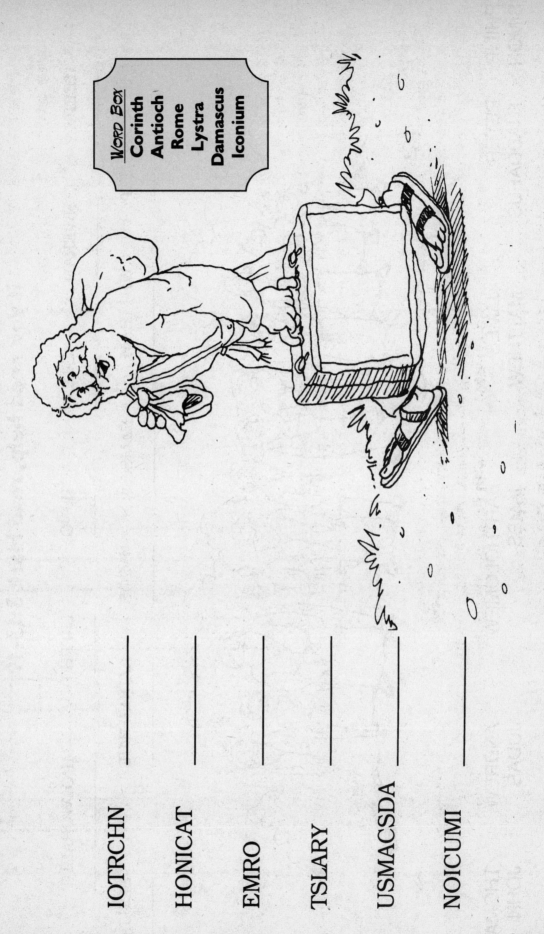

WORD BOX
Corinth
Antioch
Rome
Lystra
Damascus
Iconium

IOTRCHN _____

HONICAT _____

EMRO _____

TSLARY _____

USMACSDA _____

NOICUMI _____

After Paul became a Christian, he got excited about his faith. He spent the rest of his life traveling around telling others about Jesus.

THE CHOSEN TWELVE

Mark 3:13-19

Unscramble the words below to find out the names of Jesus' disciples. If you need help, read Mark 3:13-19.

TEEPR
_____

NWERAD
_____

SEAJM
_____

HJNO
_____

LIIPPH
_____

MEOLWORABHT
_____

MAOHST
_____

WHTTEAM
_____

EAMSJ
_____

NMIOS
_____

AADDSHTUE
_____

SDUJA
_____

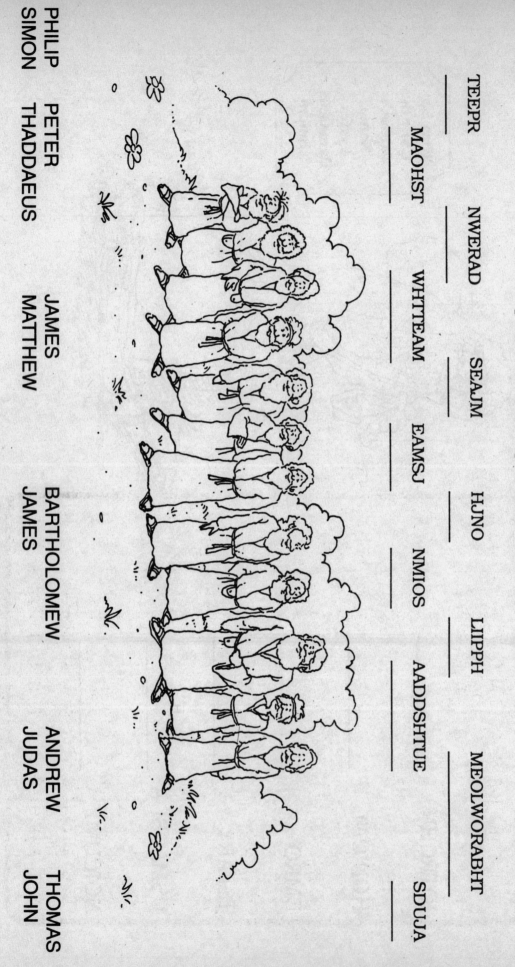

PHILIP   PETER   JAMES   BARTHOLOMEW   ANDREW   THOMAS
SIMON   THADDAEUS   MATTHEW   JAMES   JUDAS   JOHN

Jesus chose twelve men to be his special friends, called his disciples.

PAUL'S JOURNEYS

Book of Acts

See if you can find the names of the cities Paul visited in th[e]

WORD BOX
Corinth
Antioch
Ephesus
Derbe
Jerusalem
Rome
Lystra
Damascus
Philippi
Tarsus

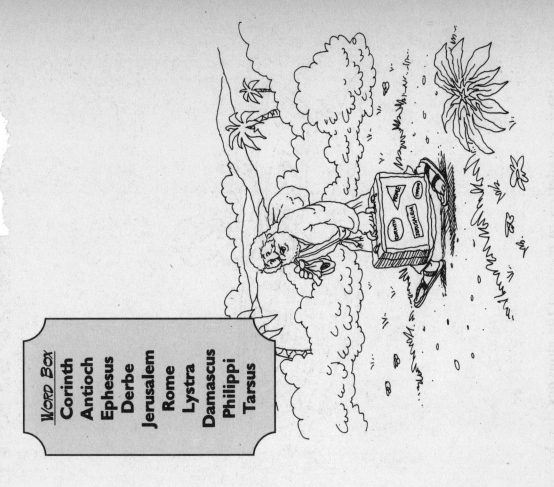

```
L J E R U S A L E M G V F D C F R
T Y T U Y V F G I D E R B E F I K
J H M N B H G P V J U L T D S A Z
X S W A E R P D F G T Y Y L P O U
J H Y N G I R E D S C V B S F R T
Y H G T L D A M A S C U S Z T S X
S X C I F R E T G B G H Y U J R I
O L H O J C O R I N T H B V E F A
T P U C T R E D F C X S W M D F G
T H Y H G F R G H J K I O L P O I
U Y T A R S U S D X S R E W Q A Z
X S D F G H Y U J H Y T G F R E D
S C X S D J H Y U I O L K I U J H
Y T F F H E P H E S U S I K L K I
```

After Paul became a Christian, he began traveling around teaching people about Jesus. He traveled to many different cities.

A SPECIAL BOOK

A rebus is several pictures where the sound of the words makes up a word. Can you figure out which book of the Bible is shown here? Write your answer below.

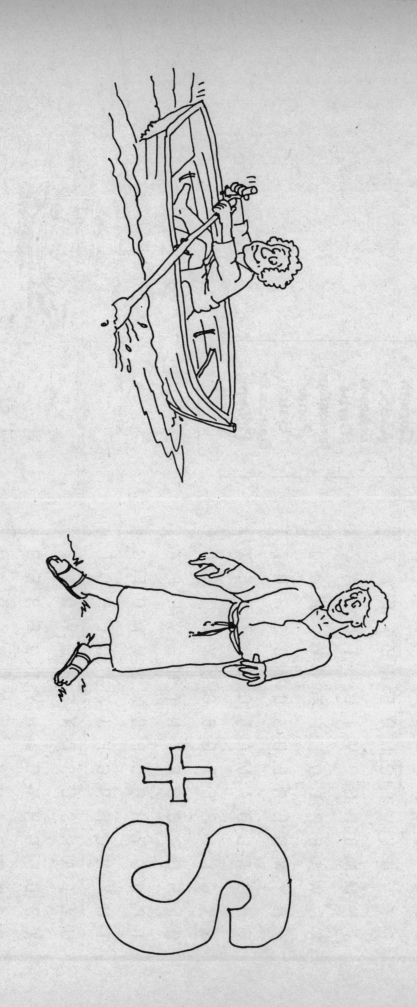

Paul wrote letters to many of the churches that he helped get started. He wrote letters to teach the churches more about God and about the right way to live. Many of those letters are now books in our Bible.

Mixed-Up Books

Unscramble these words to make the names of books in the Bible.

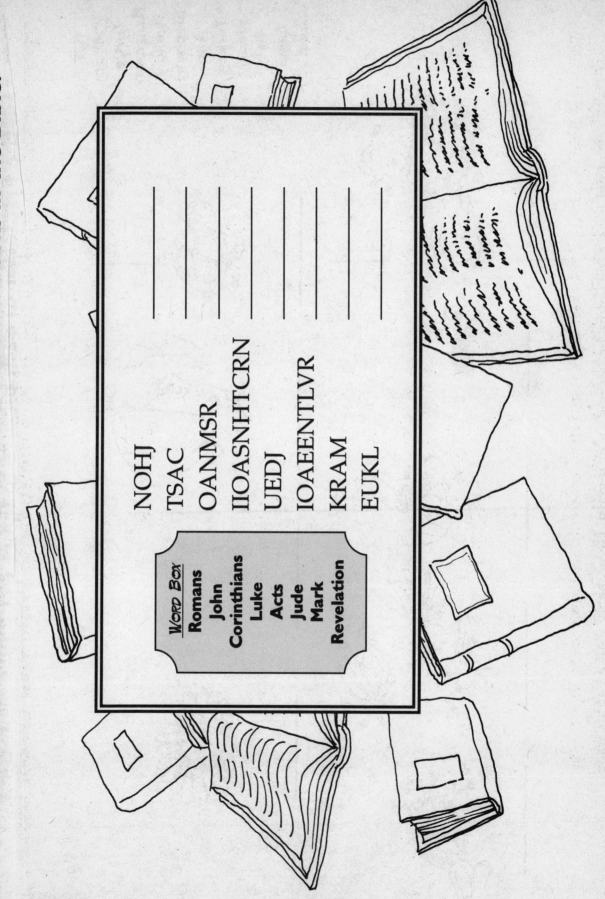

NOHJ

TSAC

OANMSR

IIOASNHTCRN

UEDJ

IOAEENTLVR

KRAM

EUKL

_____
_____
_____
_____
_____
_____
_____
_____

Word Box

Romans
John
Corinthians
Luke
Acts
Jude
Mark
Revelation

PAUL'S PROFESSION

Acts 18:3

Use the first letter of each picture to figure out Paul's profession.

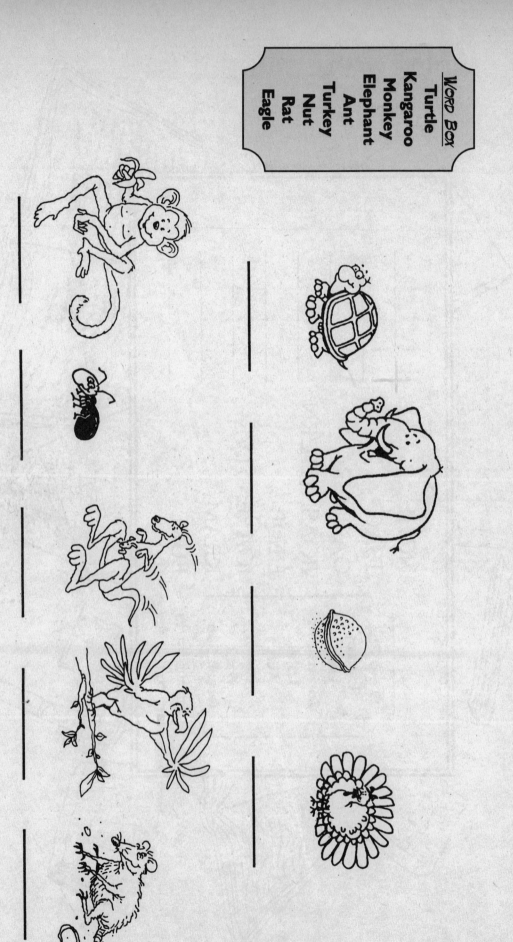

Paul did have a job before he became an evangelist. He probably worked at his trade occasionally to earn money to live on.

NEW TESTAMENT PLACES

See how many locations from New Testament times you can figure out.
Use the verses for help.

WORD BOX

Skull
Golgotha
Nazareth
Damascus
Gethsemane
Jerusalem
Egypt
Tarsus
Galilee
Bethlehem
Emmaus
Rome

Across

1. Paul was on his way to ____ when Jesus spoke to him. Acts 9:1-22
2. ____ was the city Mary and Joseph were from. Luke 2:1-7
3. Another name for Golgotha. Matthew 27:33-35
4. Paul's (Saul's) home was ____. Acts 9:11
5. The garden where Jesus prayed before he was captured. Mark 14:32
6. The Sea of ____ is where Jesus walked on water. John 6:1

Down

7. After the crucifixion Jesus appeared to the disciples on the road to ____. Luke 24:13
8. Joseph took baby Jesus and Mary to ____ for safety. Matthew 2:13-18
9. Jesus was crucified at ____. Matthew 27:33-35
10. Where Jesus was born. Matthew 2:1
11. Paul was shipwrecked on his way to ____. Acts 27:1
12. The city were Jesus was crucified. Luke 23:26-28

TOOLS OF THE TRADE

See if you can figure out which person would use which tool in the job he did. Draw a line connecting the person with their job.
Use the verses if you need help.

VERSES
1. Colossians 4:14
2. Matthew 13:53-55
3. Matthew 10:3
4. Matthew 4:18
5. Acts 18:1-5

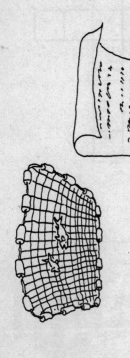

Luke

Peter

Matthew

Jesus

Paul

On a bright sunny day, Mutley was at her favorite spot on the pier, looking at the ocean. It was so big and blue! Today was going to be a wonderful day for Mutley and Gene. Gene was Mutley's best friend-the best friend a dog could ever have. Suddenly, Mutley heard barking coming from the water below. *Who's barking?* she wondered.

Mutley ran down to the bottom of the pier. *Oh, my!* she said to herself. *It's a **sea lion!*** Mutley smiled a big hello. Then she barked at the sea lion. *I'm going to see what it's like to live in the ocean today.*

Mutley went to meet Gene at the pool. Gene always took Mutley to lots of fun places. Today they were going **scuba diving!**

Gene had made special **scuba gear** for Mutley. He had given her diving lessons in a big pool.

At first, Mutley was nervous about learning to dive. Being underwater felt funny, and swimming with scuba gear felt strange. But Gene was a helpful teacher. He taught Mutley everything she needed to know.

"Good job, Mutley," he said, keeping his hand on her. "You're going to be a great **diver** in no time."

Underwater, Mutley wore a clear, plastic, **bubble helmet.** She also had a yellow **air tank** on her back. Black tubes ran from the air tank to the helmet. The tubes brought fresh air to Mutley so she could breathe underwater.

Mutley's helmet was nice and big. She could move her head around in it while she paddled here and there in the pool.

8

THIS IS TO CERTIFY THAT

MUTLEY

HAS SATISFACTORILY COMPLETED
SCUBA DIVING TRAINING
TO THE LEVEL OF
OPENWATER I
UNDER THE SANCTION OF THE
**NATIONAL ASSOCIATION
OF UNDERWATER
INSTRUCTORS**

OCEAN QUEST INTERNATIONAL

TRAINING LOCATION

Bret C. Gilliam

INSTRUCTOR SIGNATURE / NAUI NUMBER
Bret Gilliam #3234L

K9-0001

DIVER REGISTRATION NUMBER

Here is Mutley's **scuba certificate**. To earn it, she had to practice many, many hours. She is the first dog in the world ever to get one!

Now that she had earned her scuba certificate, Mutley was ready to go on her very first dive in the ocean. She and Gene put on all their scuba gear, then down, down, down they went into the deep blue ocean.

Mutley and Gene were so excited! Gene could tell that Mutley wasn't afraid, and he was right. Mutley knew Gene

would be there if she
needed help under the
water. She began barking
in her bubble helmet. *I have
a great diving partner!*

Mutley saw Gene point to a school of **Mexican goatfish.** *How beautiful they are, Mutley thought. She barked and barked. These fish don't seem to mind our being here, Gene. Let's play with them.*

12

Mutley looked all around her. She could see that the ocean was home to many kinds of sea life. And just think-it was only her first ocean dive and she had already met the Mexican goatfish. There were so many other kinds of sea life yet to meet.

Then Mutley began to wonder, *Where's my friend the sea lion? I sure hope we swim into each other!*

Suddenly Mutley began barking. Gene could see how excited she was. "What do you see, girl?" he asked Mutley.

It was another school of fish. *Oh, they're so colorful,* Mutley barked. They were silver with black-and-yellow tails. Mutley tried to swim closer to them, but they were too fast for her. They all swam away! Mutley hoped her bark had not scared them.

It wasn't long before Mutley dog-paddled into another fish. It was a **sergeant major fish,** and it swam right up to Mutley's helmet! The striped fish just stared and stared at Mutley. *I guess you've never seen a dog in scuba gear before,* thought Mutley.

Then the sergeant major fish
called over some of his fishy friends.
Mutley let out a happy bark. *Boy, these fish are staring at me, too!*
The fish had come to see the amazing underwater dog.

Mutley was so excited and barked to Gene. *Look at all the sergeant major fish there are now, Gene.* The two of them were in the middle of a giant school of fish! The sergeant majors were swimming all around Mutley, trying to get a better look.

Mutley and Gene spent a lot of time with the school of fish. Mutley even tried to count them. She used the toes on her paws to count-first the front toes, then the back ones. But then she ran out of toes! *Oh, well,* Mutley thought happily. *There are just too many sergeant majors here to count!*

As soon as Mutley and Gene left the school of sergeant majors, they swam into another school. It was more Mexican goatfish. *I know you,* Mutley barked. *You're the beautiful fish I met a little while ago.* The Mexican goatfish sure were friendly.

Mutley watched Gene begin to play with the lovely goatfish. It was a game of tag! Mutley dog-paddled over and began to play,too. She tagged so many Mexican goatfish that she wore herself out. Time for a rest!

21

What a perfect spot for a rest–a huge, underwater rock. As soon as Mutley settled on the rock to catch her breath, she looked up and saw the most magical sight. There, against the blue of the ocean, was a whole city beneath the sea.

The ocean city was made of bright-pink tree coral, and bumpy rock. Swimming all around were **cortex rainbow wrasse** fish. Mutley thought they were the most beautiful fish she had ever seen. She couldn't help but bark again and again. *What a grand day we're having, Gene!*

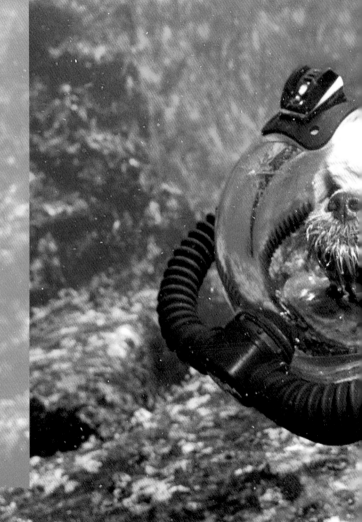

Then Mutley's day got a whole lot better. Her old friend the sea lion had found her!

"Woof, woof, woof," Mutley barked to the sea lion. *We're having a great time, sea lion. Diving is so much fun!*

Mutley, Gene, and the sea lion played together. They swam among the fish. They swam around each other. They touched hands and paws and flippers.

But soon the sea lion had to leave. He barked at Mutley and Mutley barked back. *I know, sea lion. I hope to see you again, too.*

As Mutley watched the sea lion swim away, she felt a little sad. But then she heard a soft tap on her helmet. It was Gene. He waved his hand for Mutley to follow him.

"Come with me," Gene was saying with his hand. "I have one more surprise to show you, Mutley."

Mutley was thrilled. *I'm so glad our day isn't over yet, Gene!*

Mutley dog-paddled behind Gene for a while. And then she couldn't believe her eyes. The "surprise" was thousands and thousands of fish—a huge school of **sardines,** shimmering in the sunlight. First they swooped this way, then they swooped that way. Mutley stared, then barked, then stared some more. *What amazing fish,* she thought. *What a wonderful way to end my first ocean dive!*

Gene and Mutley returned safely to land. They had loved diving together. Mutley thought to herself, *Boy, living in the ocean sure is different than living on land.* As she ran and jumped and played on the sand, she thought, *Diving in the ocean is lots of fun, but I'm really glad I'm a land animal.*

Later that afternoon, Mutley watched the sunset. She gazed out over the ocean, thinking about the new friends she and Gene had made that day. As the sun slowly set, she wondered, *What will our next adventure be? Whatever it is, I can't wait!*

Fun Facts

<u>Mutley's Scuba Gear</u>
bubble helmet
air tank
buoyancy compensator
    (see glossary)
scuba certificate

<u>Gene's Scuba Gear</u>
face mask
mouthpiece
air tank
buoyancy compensator
wet suit
fins

Gene Alba carefully made Mutley's scuba gear to make sure she would be safe and comfortable. Mutley can stay underwater up to 45 minutes. She has scuba dived up to 55 feet below the surface of the water. She and Gene have gone diving lots of different places, including the Pacific Ocean, the Atlantic Ocean, and the Caribbean.

Words About Diving

air tank   When land animals (such as people and dogs) go diving, they need to carry the air they breathe with them. That air is in a metal container called an air tank. It has enough air squeezed into it to breathe for up to 60 minutes.

bubble helmet   The special helmet, or head covering, that Gene made for Mutley. The helmet is airtight, which means air can't get out and water can't get in. Air travels from the air tank, through tubes, to Mutley's bubble helmet.

diver   A person (or dog!) who swims underwater. Very often, divers wear scuba gear so they can stay underwater a long time.

scuba certificate   The special piece of paper given to scuba divers to say they have practiced enough on their own to go diving by themselves.

scuba diving To swim underwater with the help of scuba gear. The word "scuba" is really an abbreviation. That means s-c-u-b-a is short for self-contained underwater breathing apparatus.

scuba gear   The different tools scuba divers use to dive. For people, scuba gear includes a face mask, mouthpiece, air tank, wet suit, and fins. Mutley's gear included a bubble helmet and an air tank. All divers also wear a buoyancy compensator, which is used to help the divers either float or sink.

Sea Life

cortex rainbow wrasse   A small fish usually 6 to 12 inches in length, found in rocky areas of the Pacific Ocean.

Mexican goatfish   A small tropical fish found in the Pacific Ocean, near the country of Mexico.

sardine A very small, silvery fish found in all the oceans of the world. Sardines swim in huge schools. They are tasty. People catch and eat them.

sea lion A kind of seal that lives in the Pacific Ocean. Sea lions are different than fur seals. They're bigger, and they don't have the furry undercoat fur seals have.

sergeant major fish   A small striped fish usually 6 to 8 inches in length, found in shallow reefs of the Pacific Ocean.